Bitcoin & Cryptocurrency Investing:

Top 10 DeFi Altcoins to Change the World and Your Finances, Blockchain, Cold Storage, NFT & Mining Explained, Smart Contracts & Decentralized Finance for Swing Trading

D1640337

"We see bitcoin as potentially the greatest social network of all."
~ Tyler Winklevoss

been made to provide accurate, up to date and reliable complete

information. No warranties of any kind are expressed or implied. Readers acknowledge that the author is not engaging in the rendering of legal, financial, medical or professional advice. The content of this book has been derived from various sources. Please consult a licensed professional before attempting any techniques outlined in this book.

By reading this document, the reader agrees that under no circumstances are is the author responsible for any losses, direct or indirect, which are incurred as a result of the use of information contained within this document, including, but not limited to, —errors, omissions, or inaccuracies.

Table of contents

Introduction

"To make our world a better place, we need to build products that the corrupt cannot abuse. Bitcoin is the best example of that."

- Olawale Daniel-

Just mention Bitcoin in a conversation and you'll be hearing varied opinions from people around you. Why there is a fuss over this cryptocurrency? What makes it a hot topic that can stir contrasting views? How well do you know Bitcoin-it's history, uses, benefits, and journey to the top of the crypto list?

Let me give you insights and answers about Bitcoin through this book. **Bitcoin & Cryptocurrency Investing: Top 10 DeFi Altcoins to Change the World and Your Finances, Blockchain, Cold Storage, NFT & Mining Explained, Smart Contracts & Decentralized Finance for Swing Trading** is not your ordinary book.

It is your ticket to understand Bitcoin and leverage its features to achieve your investing goals. This is a no-holds-barred journey to Bitcoin crypto investing, so feel free to navigate and explore each chapter that is designed to help you understand Bitcoin better. It tackles the fundamentals of Bitcoin as well as strategies, tips, and information to guide you through the complex world of pure crypto and bitcoin-related stock investing.

Take note that while it will help you navigate cryptocurrency investing, this book does not guarantee your financial success. It is just a means, a journal of tips and strategies to help you gain confidence and knowledge on how to pursue Bitcoin investing. Your success in investing is in your hands. It is about knowing the right timing, the right asset vehicle, when to buy or sell your holdings, and a whole lot more.

Every investor wants profits, whether direct or passive income. When we buy something, we expect to get hold of a commodity we like, need, or want. In crypto investing, we pay for a virtual commodity with a value that rests on the users' adoption of its worth. Crypto investing, especially in Bitcoin, requires a strong might and risk tolerance.

If you want a "safe investment" that brings in guaranteed returns, do not invest in cryptocurrency especially Bitcoin. It is not an appropriate asset for those who do not like risks, because in just a fleeting moment, a significant downtrend in the market, you could lose a great portion of your invested fund.

But Bitcoin investing offers a path that can make you an overnight millionaire or even a billionaire, depending on the number of coins you have in your personal portfolio. Bitcoin remains a volatile, high-risk asset. But its volatility makes this crypto one of the most interesting, powerful, and profitable investment assets.

For conservative investors, Bitcoin investing is an attractive option but they hesitate on trying this option due to the risks and uncertainties that its nature brings. However, with the increasing growth of institutional and big investors, the level of hesitancy is beginning to wane. The crypto industry is evolving and is now connecting with the traditional forms of investment through Bitcoin-linked exchange-traded funds (ETFs) and crypto stocks of major companies. While indirectly, investors enjoy the opportunity of tasting the power of Bitcoin.

Bitcoin follows the principles of market efficiency and principles of economics. While it runs independently with its own technology, rules, and principles, it has shown liquidity, security, fungibility, and sustainability. The fact that its supply would be limited does not discourage investors but only makes it more interesting in their eyes. Indeed, Bitcoin has grown so much in terms of public acceptance, the number of loyal users and holders, and returns of investment. From an uncertain beginning, Bitcoin showed its strength and flexibility despite the price spikes and crashes. It always recovers from a bearish period with a higher price baseline and continues to dominate the crypto scene.

Bitcoin is a trailblazer that inspires creators to make their own cryptocurrency and spawns crypto-related projects. This alone makes it a powerful asset vehicle and currency in this modern world where the internet makes everything possible. It still has a lot of room to grow and potentials to explore.

More than 10 years ago, Bitcoin does not possess any real monetary value. But look at it now, one bitcoin is more than the value of one dollar or any fiat currency. It is like gold that holds such a large value, even without physical form. It is just a concept in the digital sphere, but because users embrace its speculative value, it has grown so much bigger.

Satoshi Nakamoto, the person behind this project is truly a man of vision. He has created one of the best inventions in the 21st century. His legacy is tantamount to the future of the financial world and the future is beginning right now. Bitcoin has opened the door for another gold rush- this time in digital form. Its raucous journey has turned ordinary people into wealthy ones and rich people losing a lot of money due to not-so-smart investment moves.

History showed that it took four pieces of bitcoins to make a penny. This was what happened during the first Bitcoin transaction when Laszlo Hanyecz bought 2 Papa John's pizzas in Florida for $25 or equivalent to 10,000 bitcoins. Today, to get hold of 1 bitcoin, you need to pay thousands of dollars.

While it is waiting for the time where its primary purpose will come true- as a medium to pay for daily transactions just like the fiat currencies, Bitcoin has already gained traction as a hedge against inflation and a store of value. While Bitcoin's price is still highly-volatile, the trust of institutional investors and attempts of regulatory agencies to make applicable rules are making the crypto market more mature.

The narrative also changed. In the past, the price fluctuations stemmed from the speculative moves of traders and retail investors. Nowadays, the market price of Bitcoin is influenced by a set of factors in the mainstream economy.

This book **Bitcoin & Cryptocurrency Investing: Top 10 DeFi Altcoins to Change the World and Your Finances, Blockchain, Cold Storage, NFT & Mining Explained, Smart Contracts & Decentralized Finance for Swing Trading** will take you on a journey and teach you how to effectively invest in Bitcoin. Each chapter is written to enlighten, prepare, and help you master the strategies of crypto investing.

Chapter 1 Hail to the King of Crypto: Bitcoin gives you the birds-eye view of the hottest cryptocurrency, how it works, its unique characteristics, and more.

Chapter 2 The Digital Gold Rush gives you a list of people who trusted and enjoyed the perks of investing in Bitcoin as well as the countries that accept it and forbid its trading plus a whole lot more.

Chapter 3 Is Crypto Investing for You? talks about the principles of crypto investing, the risks and rewards, and how its operating system blockchain works to your advantage.

Chapter 4 Bitcoin and Stock Market explains the correlation between Bitcoin and the stock market, the successful journey of bitcoin futures to the traditional trading markets, and the preview of crypto stocks to invest in before the next digital rush.

Chapter 5 Guide to Bitcoin Investing: Let's Gear You Up teaches you how to buy and sell Bitcoin, top reasons why and why you should not invest, ways and strategies to invest, and other investing concepts you can use along the way.

Chapter 6 Personal Portfolio Management helps you understand the benefits of a well-managed, diversified portfolio, the investment styles to use, factors to consider, how to manage your own portfolio, or hire a portfolio manager.

Chapter 7 What Should Comprise Your Crypto Portfolio? allows you to choose what to include in your portfolio, how to optimize the crypto evolution (Bitcoin, Ethereum, and DeFi), and pick the perfect asset for you from the top 10

DeFi altcoins that are making an impact on the world's financial sectors.

Chapter 8 Everything You Need to Ask About Bitcoin & Resources for Bitcoin Investors answers your questions about Bitcoin. There is also a list of the most useful resources for everyone who wants to invest in Bitcoin.

As the author of this book, I used my more than ten years of experience as well my share of failures and successes to produce this book. I was like you once- a beginner who kept reading, trying, positioning, finding the right asset vehicle, and believing that I can master the art of investing. I can proudly say that I found my pot of gold in investing and I want to guide you through this book.

It is my pay it forward gesture. I want you to know the key secrets of successful investors. All it takes is to open the first page and continue learning until the last page.

This book is for you. Press on.

Chapter 1

Hail to the King of Crypto: Bitcoin

"Bitcoin is a techno tour de force." – *Bill Gates*

In the span of more than 10 years, Bitcoin becomes a household name. But not all people know how it works, how it can be used for global transactions via the internet, and why it has become a new investment and trading craze.

In laymen's terms, Bitcoin refers to the digital currency that operates on its own blockchain system. It survives without the traditional backing of precious metals or fiat currency. It trades on exchange platforms and uses electronic wallets or hardware wallets for safekeeping purposes.

For beginners and casual investors, delving deeper than its face value is very important. The basics are relatively easy to comprehend. Let me take you on the journey of learning about Bitcoin, the most valuable cryptocurrency on the world's virtual markets today.

1. Bitcoin is an electronic representation of money that uses cryptography for verifying its transaction. Cryptography refers to the science of encoding and decoding details and information.

2. Bitcoin as an investment asset that offers inflation hedge and capital appreciation. However, the volatile nature of its market value makes long-term investment high-risk.

3. Bitcoin is a digital, decentralized, private, and scarce resource. It operates according to its set of codes. Its code is being run and processed by nodes or thousands of high-end computers across the globe. It is used for transactions without the intervention of a bank or middleman. Bitcoin code is limited to 21 million only.

Satoshi Nakamoto: The father of Bitcoin

The concept and development of Bitcoin are credited to Satoshi Nakamoto. But who's he, anyway? Until today, the real identity of the father of bitcoin remains elusive. Some speculated that the name was just a pseudonym of a person or a group of people behind the cryptocurrency.

Nakamoto authored the whitepaper of Bitcoin and designed the blockchain database among other things. His goal in creating this cryptocurrency is to put the control of currency in the people's hands and take it away from powerful financial elites.

He was active during the introduction of Bitcoin, then went off the radar after three years. His co-developer Gavin Andersen received a farewell email on April 23, 2011, saying that Nakamoto "moved on to other things" and that he knew that Bitcoin's future was in 'good hands.' Nakamoto assigned Andersen as the caretaker of Bitcoin. As of today, Andersen is getting more reclusive and has also given up his role as 'a core maintainer' of the Bitcoin code.

Trivia

Gavin Andersen wrote code for Bitcoin during its inception and became Satoshi Nakamoto's trusted right-hand associate.

And while Nakamoto is "out there doing other things", he is enjoying profits from his own share of bitcoins. He owns more than 1 million Bitcoins which is worth around $60 billion based on the current (2021) market price. His coins also equate to 5% of the total circulating bitcoins.

If Nakamoto sells part of his million coins, it would totally upend the entire crypto market.

Attempts to unmask Nakamoto

Mystery fires the active and wild imagination of people. When Nakamoto preferred to remain hidden while developing Bitcoin, many speculations and guesses surrounded him. There were rumors about him being a Yakuza member, a money launderer, or a participant of a cabal of programmers and developers. Some people even thought that he is a woman.

His mask of anonymity ignited many attempts to reveal his true identity. Some of the personalities that were associated with Nakamoto's persona include:

- One of the 'suspects' was Nick Szabo, a crypto expert who helped Nakamoto develop Bitcoin. The New York Times pinned him as Nakamoto, but he denied the claim. Some linguists even studied and compared his writings with

Nakamoto's and believed that there were some semblances.

- In 2014, Newsweek identified Dorian Nakamoto as the man behind Bitcoin because of his successful engineering career and partly because of having the same surname. The publication also claimed that both Nakamotos have Japanese connections and lean on libertarian beliefs. Dorian strongly denied his involvement with cryptocurrency by issuing a public statement via the Associated Press. The next day, the 'mystery man' Nakamoto posted a brief statement in an online forum saying "I am not Dorian Nakamoto."

- When Australian scientist Craig Wright announced in 2016 that he was Nakamoto, the crypto community didn't believe him. He even presented academic credentials and references to the crypto paper that appeared on his own blog months before the Bitcoin whitepaper appeared online. In addition, there were also references about leaked correspondence and emails about "P2P distributed ledger" with his lawyers. But inconsistencies in his proofs became the subject of criticisms. Even when Bitcoin co-developer Andersen backed Wright's claim by saying that he was '98% sure', there was lots of backlash. Eventually, Wright retreated.

How well do you know Bitcoin?

Bitcoin is a cryptocurrency that utilizes cryptology to secure its system. It is a decentralized virtual currency that is created (mined), distributed, stored, and traded using a ledger system known as the blockchain.

Its decade of history of value is marked with cycles of impressive booms and turbulent crashes. Investors and traders watched in awe as Bitcoin's value soared high and then crashed down. Nevertheless, the volatility of this crypto did not stop the widespread popularity that inspired the creation of many alternative coins (altcoins).

Early timeline

August 18, 2008 – Bitcoin.org was registered. At present, this domain name is "WhoisGuardProtected." This means that the identification of the entity or entities that registered the name is private and confidential information.

October 31, 2008 – Satoshi Nakamoto sent a statement at metzdowd.com's Cryptography Mailing list that he has been working on a fully peer-to-peer electronic cash system. According to him, this new project would not require a trusted third party to operate. This information was included in the whitepaper entitled "Bitcoin: A Peer-to-Peer Electronic Cash System", which can be accessed on bitcoin.org. It is the Magna Carta of bitcoin's operation then and now.

January 3, 2009 – This date marked the mining of the first bitcoin block- Block 0 or the 'genesis block.' Written in the block was the message "The Times 03/Jan/2009 Chancellor on brink of second bailout for banks." The context of the statement has puzzled the public.

Only Yakamoto and his peers knew its relevance.

January 8, 2009 – Bitcoin mining and operation officially began when Block 1 was mined.

Bitcoin mining

Bitcoin is produced through mining or the process where this crypto is released for circulation. The term mining in bitcoin is a reference to the method of gathering precious metals or the digital equivalent of finding cryptocurrency. The idea is akin to finding gold where anyone with a shovel can dig and look for it. In bitcoin mining, people with computer skills and knowledge can participate and look for blocks.

Crypto miners can join the network as transaction processors and validators. They need to solve complex puzzles to unlock new blocks. Using specialized computer hardware in computing difficult mathematical problems, miners need to complete the task and produce a 'hash' (64-character output) that will lock the new block to the network.

The new blocks are important elements in adding, verifying, and storing transaction records in the Bitcoin network. Each block on the blockchain network represents a file that can store 1MB of bitcoin transactions. On December 13, 2020, the blockchain size was already 308 gigabytes (GB).

The first miners to add new blocks to the blockchain earn bitcoins. To get the reward, miners should prove their role as a blockchain network through PoW or proof of work system. The proof of effort should include the energy and time spent to run their computers and solve the equations. The faster and more high-end the hardware of computers, the larger yields of block rewards they would receive.

Companies that are built for mining use specially-designed computer chips to process Bitcoin transactions and earn rewards. Large transactions that involve greater monetary value need more validations to guarantee security.

Did you know that?

The Bitcoin mining farms across the globe consume approximately 60 terawatt-hours of electricity every year.

Bitcoin halving

Bitcoin halving, as the phrase implies, is a major event where the coin incentives of miners are cut in half or reduced to 50% after reaching the 210,000 newly-discovered blocks quota. It aims to ensure that the circulating amount of bitcoin would not trigger pressure for exponential increase of market price.

The halving occurs every four years and will continue until the last batch of 210,000 bitcoins is mined. After mining the last block, expect Bitcoin to be more scarce and valuable.

During the initial stage of Bitcoin in 2009, the reward for miners was 50 BTC.

- The first halving happened in 2012, cutting down the incentive to 25 BTC for every block mined.
- The second halving occurred in 2016, slashing the reward to 12.5 BTC and completing 420,000 blocks.
- The third halving was on May 11, 2020, where miners earned 6.25 BTC for each block they unlocked. It marked the completion of unlocking 630,000 blocks.
- The fourth halving is expected to happen in 2024, considering that new coins are generated every 10 minutes.

- The final halving is predicted to take place between 2040 and 2140.

Consequently, halving brings dramatic effects because it often triggers a significant Bitcoin turbulence. It is characterized by surges in trading volume 1 month before and 1 month after every halving. Understandably, when halving is happening, there is a short supply of Bitcoin in the market. The law of demand and supply dictates that when there is not enough supply, the price of the asset will increase, In the case of Bitcoin, the value of the coins yet to be produced is expected to be higher.

- The history of Bitcoin halving showed that on November 28, 2012, the price per BTC was around $12 then skyrocketed after a year to around $1,217.

- When the second halving happened on July 9, 2016, the value of Bitcoin was $670 and then rose to $2,550 per BTC by July 2017. The price continued to rise and by December 2017, Bitcoin's market price peaked at an all-time high of $19,700 per coin. In December 2018, it fell down to $3,276, which was 506% higher than its pre-halving price.

- The third halving took place at around 3 PM EST on May 11, 2020. The price per Bitcoin was $8,787. Several weeks later, Bitcoin surpassed all its all-time highs and set its bull-run performance on February 21 with over $58,000 per coin price. But, it didn't stop there as the price soared to an astonishing $64,507 per BTC, which was 634% higher than its pre-halving value. On May 11, 2021, it settled to $54,276 (517% higher than the 2016 halving).

The diminishing rate of miners' subsidies is pre-determined by Nakamoto. It revolves around the idea that as the transaction fees in the network increase, the reward for discovering a newly-minted coin shall be decreased. Technically, this key feature of Bitcoin helps control crypto inflation and emission. Within the Bitcoin code lies the automatic adjustment in releasing new crypto coins, which consequently postpone the end date of emission.

Interestingly, there were two events that resulted in further Bitcoin price fluctuation. First, when Tesla CEO Elon Musk announced on May 12, 2021, that his company would not be accepting Bitcoin payments. The second event that plunged down the price below $40,000 was the restrictions imposed by Chinese regulators, banning payment firms and financial institutions from offering crypto-related services. These two announcements caused Bitcoin price drop.

Crypto experts in the industry viewed the recent halving as a robust factor that can impact its ecosystem in many ways. One of them is the decreasing number of miners because the economic mining rewards are getting smaller. It makes Bitcoin mining less compelling and unprofitable for efficient miners.

After the final halving, all Bitcoin miners will receive incentives in the form of transaction fees from people who sell and buy the crypto. This is to ensure continuous processing on the blockchain. As of August 2021, the circulating bitcoins were 18,799,131 million. It means that only 2,200, 869 million coins are waiting to be mined.

Trivia
Did you know that there is a micro-nation with bitcoin as its currency? It is the Liberland, a place between Serbia and Croatia. It was founded in April 2015 by Vit Jedlicka.

Blockchain: The core of Bitcoin operation

Bitcoin exists within blockchain technology. It was the first cryptocurrency that successfully used the innovative system of recording key information. To date, the Bitcoin blockchain application is still the best in the crypto industry.

Although in terms of scalability, it is relatively slow because Bitcoin blockchain can only process up to 7 new transactions per second. Its competitor Ethereum can process 30 every second while the Visa credit card system can complete 24,000 transactions per second.

People are also looking forward to the much-anticipated upgraded version of Ethereum or Ethereum 2.0, which is expected to handle up to 10,000 transactions per second.

In essence, blockchain refers to the trustless, transparent, and publicly accessible transaction ledger in the bitcoin network that allows ownership transfer using proof of work (PoW) and public-key encryption. It is a type of digital ledger of transactions (DLT) where inputs are duplicated, distributed, and validated across the whole computer network.

This public ledger is maintained by many computers across the globe. This network of state-of-the-art computers validates, encrypts, and stores transactions in blocks. The growing blocks as transactions continue are linked together with the use of cryptography. Recording of completed transactions requires the use of hash or cryptographic signature.

Why makes blockchain technology interesting?

It is one of the 21ˢᵗ most-hyped systems that was developed by Nakamoto to support Bitcoin's digital operation. At present, it has many versions to power altcoins. Developers are also integrating blockchain technology into different industries and businesses that need automated authorization, legal contracts, and records of transaction series.

Its secure and innovative features resolve trust issues. Since no one is running the bitcoin blockchain in terms of administration, all users are the ones who are making it active. No one can directly steal your coins unless you send them to a fraud person who is doing virtual business with you. In this case, it would be impossible to retrieve the fund you sent and the only one who can withdraw the money is the other party.

Another reason for the hype around this technology is its capability to prevent your bitcoins from being hacked, double-spent, or faked.

What are the properties of blockchain technology?

- **Distributed** – Network participants receive a copy of the digital ledger, ensuring the transparency of transactions.

- **Programmable** – It is programmable for a certain purpose with the help of Smart Contracts for transactions.

- **Anonymous** – The identity of users is either pseudonymous or anonymous.

- **Unanimous** – All the participants of the blockchain network agree to the validity of transactions.

- **Secure** – To ensure security, all records of transactions are individually encrypted.

- **Immutable** – All validated records cannot be reversed and changed.

- **Time-stamped** - The timestamp of every transaction is recorded permanently on the block.

The growing blocks on the blockchain significantly enhance the ledger's security. It means that if hackers attempt to tamper information or corrupt the entire system, they need to change all the blocks across the distributed versions in various locations.

Also, when one network participant sees tampered information, it would automatically halt the process and send it back as an error or invalid transaction.

How does Bitcoin Blockchain work?

Step 1: The sale or purchase of bitcoin is entered into the system, then transmitted to the thousands of nodes (network of computers).

Step 2: Each of these nodes would have its turn to confirm the validity of the transaction based on computer algorithms. The participant (or miner) who successfully produces a new block for the fresh transaction is rewarded with the transaction fee that the buyer or seller pays.

The fees vary according to the volume of purchased or sold bitcoins.

Step 3: Once the transaction is cryptographically validated and affirmed by the majority of the nodes, the sale will be encrypted to a block on the digital ledger.

Step 4: The block where the data is encrypted will be permanently chained to the previous blocks after using a hash (cryptographic fingerprint).

Peer-to-Peer (P2P) Network

In the Bitcoin network, the full nodes aka peers work with others to give essence to the peer-to-peer protocol for block and transaction exchange. It means that users can receive or send payments from other users on the network regardless of their locations. The transactions are purely P2P or do not need the approval of external authority or source unless they are doing business with a regulated institution or exchange.

Full nodes are capable of downloading and verifying each block and transaction before sending them to other nodes in the blockchain. There are two types of full nodes:

> ➢ Archival nodes – These are full nodes with the ability to serve historical blocks to their peers as well as store the whole blockchain.

➤ Pruned nodes- They are full nodes that do not have the ability to store the whole blockchain.

How does P2P operate?

Before a single full node can start validating a freshly-mined block and unconfirmed user transaction, it must be downloaded first and validate all existing blocks from block 1 to the last block in the network chain. This process is known as the Initial Block Download (IBD), where the node downloads all the previous blocks to prepare for the new transaction.

When a miner unlocks a new block, he can use either of the following methods to broadcast his successful discovery.

- **Standard Block Relay** – It is the approach where the miner acts as the relay node. It will send an "inv" (inventory) message to peers (full nodes and SPV). The inventory refers to the newly discovered block.

  The common responses of the peers include *"getdata"* message from block-first (BF) peer which means it is requesting the whole block, *"getheaders"* message from headers-first (HF) peer that also wants the full block, or *"getdata"* message from SPV (Simplified

Payment Verification) user who wants a Merkle block.

The miner responds to every request by sending the new block according to the type of message its peers like "block" message, "headers" message, or "merkleblock" message then adding zero or more "tx" messages. The "tx" message contains a transaction in raw format.

- **Unsolicited Block Push** – The miner will send a *"block"* message to all full node peers. In this approach, it bypasses the standard block relay method knowing that none of the full nodes has the newly-discovered bitcoin block.

For sending transactions to its peer, the full node will use an "inv" message. The receiving peer will forward it to the next node in the same format.

Bitcoin forks

Bitcoin forks are the changes in the network's protocol or when 2 or more blocks display the same block height. When Bitcoin forks, it generates a new coin or token as well as a new network. This impacts the validity of the old rules, forcing miners to adapt to the new rules.

It also occurs when developers:

- disagree on the best way to handle Bitcoin's growth forward
- reverse catastrophic or hacking bugs
- add new features to the blockchain

The main classification of forks:

- **Hard fork** – A bitcoin hard fork is a radical change to the blockchain's protocol, resulting in 2 branches. One follows the protocol, while the other one becomes a new version. The forking process would upgrade the software rules and the mining procedures, causing the invalidation of new transactions.

  Hard forking needs consensus from the majority of coin holders to push through. For its adoption, there should be enough nodes to update to the newest version. Those who prefer not to update lose access to the new blockchain.

- **Soft fork** – A soft fork is a subtle modification in the software protocol and does not generate a new currency. It is also called UASF or a user-activated soft fork. It occurs by users' initiation instead of the miners or supercomputers who maintain the Bitcoin network.

  The user would adopt a specific action on how to interact with the blockchain. If other users follow suit and there is an adequate number, a fork follows.

During the forking process, new digital currencies are created with names similar to the mother crypto.

Examples are the following:

- **Bitcoin Cash (B cash**) – It was the first new coin that Bitcoin forking has created in August 2017. Its creation was a historical moment for Bitcoin and the whole crypto community. Bitcoin Cash is the 11th cryptocurrency in terms of market cap and is one of the most successful hard forks from its primary cryptocurrency. It offers 8 megabytes blocks.

The Bitcoin Cash network has a hard fork that produced Bitcoin Satoshi's Vision (SBV). It was a project of Craig Wright, one of the noted individuals who claimed that he is Satoshi Nakamoto.

- **Bitcoin Gold** – This bitcoin was another result of a hard fork that happened in October 2017. The developers behind the hard fork felt that the mining functionality has become specialized in terms of hardware and equipment so they restored the basic graphics processing units (GPUs).

  Bitcoin Gold uses a pre-mine process, generating 100,000 coins as an aftermath of the fork. Most of these coins were in a 'special endowment' designed to help the future growth and financing of the Bitcoin Gold ecosystem as well as payment for miners.

- **Bitcoin Diamond** – Its objective is to enable cheaper and faster Bitcoin transactions.

- **Bitcoin Private** – The goal is to keep the transactions of users totally confidential or private.

Other notable forks of Bitcoin include:

- **Bitcoin XT** – This was the first significant bitcoin hard fork. It was launched in 2014 by Mike Hearn to include the new features he proposed like increasing the size of the block from 1 to 8 megabytes. It would mean processing 24 transactions every second instead of 7 transactions. In 2015, the software was running 1,000 nodes but was later abandoned by users due to disinterest.

- **Bitcoin Classic** – In 2016, another attempt to increase the block size was done by a group of developers. It ran 2,000 nodes after its launching but lost the majority of users who chose different options. It still exists and is supported by several developers.

- **Bitcoin Unlimited** – Another project was launched in 2016, the Bitcoin Unlimited. But while the developers of this project have released the code, they did not specify the kind of fork it needs. This fork gave users options to choose the size of the blocks up to 16 megabytes. It failed to gain positive users' acceptance.

Bitcoin clones

Not every fork results in a new cryptocurrency. There are software splits that copy the underlying code. Clones are technically not forks, but they are usually called 'forks' because they cloned the source code of Bitcoin, then began anew.

- **Litecoin (LTC)** – Considered the first clone of Bitcoin was initiated in 2011 by Charlie Lee. Its primary goal was to become the "silver" to Bitcoin's gold status. Instead of using the SHA-256 algorithm of Bitcoin, it follows the Scrypt algorithm. After several years, it had its own hard fork and produced Litecoin Cash.

- **Vertcoin** (VTC) – This Bitcoin clone aimed to leverage the mining process by keeping the mining resistant against Application-Specific Integrated Circuit (ASIC).

How did Bitcoin forks or clones affect the crypto community?

Forks, particularly hard forks, create a level of disruption in the community of users. The competing visions of developers usually make the miners, traders, and investors feel that they have no other choice but to make a decision to separate ways. More often, the fractured community would engage in heated debates and controversies. If there is too much disruption over the plan, it can prevent the fork from taking place.

This was the case with SegWit 2. X, a 2017 fork project. It didn't push through because of 'insufficient consensus for a clean upgrade of the blocksize'. Many feared that the upsize plan would create another hard fork and cause Bitcoin destabilization.

In relation to cloning the blockchain, there is a huge possibility that whale investors would try to purchase all the available tokens, knowing that they would cost more after the production of the new coin. This create artificial inflation of price and demand for the parent currency until the day of the cloning.

After the successful cloning, the whales have in their possession new tokens and parent tokens. Their next move is to dump them most of the crypto on crypto exchanges, causing a crash of value for the parent and forked token.

Unique characteristics of Bitcoin

User autonomy

Unlike the traditional fiat currencies that are vulnerable to external factors like economic crisis or major political developments, Bitcoin stands on its own. Its value is not affected by the usual problems in society or certain government policies. Only the holders and users of this cryptocurrency control the coins.

Pseudonymous

Users are not required to send personal information for identification purposes. The user can use a blockchain address to identify himself. The Bitcoin network also allows users to have multiple addresses in marking various transactions.

Immutable

All stored transactions in the blockchain of Bitcoin are irreversible. They cannot be altered or amended by any third party like a financial service agency, bank authority, or government entity. But if you mistakenly send a bitcoin to someone, you cannot file a charge bank. Your coin is gone forever unless the recipient returns the original bitcoin out of goodwill.

Secure

Since bitcoin is a virtual currency, there are fewer threat of theft. The only way to steal crypto is when a hacker knows the private keys of the user's electronic wallet. But in general, it is impossible to steal the coins. Up to this day, Bitcoin's blockchain remains secure to breaches and hacking, ensuring that transactions between two or multiple addresses are safe.

Low transaction fees

For international transactions, the service fees of Bitcoin are comparatively lower than conventional wire transfers. The standard methods usually have services costs and other fees. Bitcoin eliminates intermediaries and advocates direct transactions between the sender and receiver, making it a more hassle-free and cost-saving alternative. Moreover, transferring funds is faster due to the absence of a waiting period and authorization requirement.

Accessible

The power is in the hands of users. The ease of accessing bitcoins and using them for global transactions makes Bitcoin a must-have currency in this modern world. With only a computer or a smartphone, users can send or receive funds wherever they are. It empowers people who have no access to the banking system, credit cards, and other traditional modes of payment.

Mobile

As long as your device has Internet access, you can pay for your purchases or send/receive bitcoins wherever your location is. You don't have to go to the nearest bank to complete the transaction or visit a store to pay for the product. And what's more important is you don't have to supply your personal information to complete the online transaction.

Guide to storing BTC

Bitcoin needs a digital wallet. This wallet stores the bitcoins and the private keys that correspond to the blockchain address of the user. These keys are in the form of cryptographic information that helps you access your funds and transact business with another user.

Technically, a Bitcoin wallet is a program or device that is created for easy interaction with the blockchain. It is synonymous with a physical wallet, but instead of physical forms of money, it stores a set of private numbers (private keys) that unlocks the blockchain address of the user. When you sign in for Bitcoin transactions, you need to use these private keys to prove that you are the owner of the coins. It is crucial to keep your private keys confidential to prevent attackers from opening your address and move your bitcoins to their own wallets.

There are several types of Bitcoin wallets to match your needs. Each is different from each other in terms of accessibility, convenience, security, and other features. For instance, the full-node wallets support the Bitcoin network's decentralized nature. There are also mobile wallets with built-in QR code scanners or integrated crypto exchanges for convenient buying and selling of coins.

Types of Bitcoin wallets

- **Mobile wallets** –This type of wallet is an app that runs on the smartphone with private keys, making it virtually easy and quick to access the bitcoins. It is best for users who use Bitcoin for their daily transactions like trading and purchasing goods from retailers who accept crypto payments. Mobile wallet uses simplified payment verification (SPV) technology and relies on the Bitcoin network's trusted nodes for correct information.

The downside of mobile wallets is their vulnerability to hacking and malware issues. To prevent them from occurring, always enable the 2-factor authentication feature of your device and app. If you want a more secure authenticator app that is not prone to email hacks or SIM swap attacks, try FreeOTP, Authy, or Google Authenticator.

- **Web wallets** – Web wallets are online wallets of exchange platforms and are controlled by a broker/third party. They have several features that allow you to replicate your address across the devices you often use or link them to your desktop and mobile wallets. Like mobile wallets, web wallets allow users to access their Bitcoins while on the go.

  However, the people running the exchange platform have total control of your funds because they have access to your account's private keys. Another downside of using a web wallet is the risk of leaked emails and passwords which are half of your login credentials to access the funds.

- **Desktop wallets** – They are downloadable wallets that can be installed on your computer device. The private keys to access your bitcoins are stored on the hard drive or SSD. Compared to web and mobile wallets, desktop wallets are more secure because you have total control over your funds. But because they are accessible using the web, there is still a big risk. This wallet, however, is ideal for people who trade a little amount of BTC using their computers.

If you choose to use a wallet with full nodes, you need large disk space and a quick internet connection. This kind of wallet offers granular control that other wallets lack.

  ✓ It delivers optimum performance by broadcasting the transactions directly to the system's memory pool.
  ✓ It features a replace-by-fee checkbox that lets you increase the transaction fees to make the transaction quicker.
  ✓ It has CLI and API in the interface, allowing app developers to incorporate the Bitcoin-related

functionalities in the apps they use or build a proprietary wallet of their own.

✓ It comes with an intuitive drop-down box with speed control and transaction fee.

- **Paper Wallet**s – They are physical documents containing the public address where users can receive Bitcoin and the private key to enable transferring coins in the address. They are like QR-codes that you need to scan before adding the wallet keys to start a transaction. If you want to print the generated keys as a backup, store them in a safe place.

- **Hardware wallets** – They are also called **cold storage**. These are physical devices that securely store the private keys to your crypto account. They are regarded as the safest storage for Bitcoin and have immunity against computer viruses. When picking a hardware wallet, look for the brand with a screen that displays and verifies the wallet details. The screen serves as another layer of protection because it can confirm the address and amount of payment you will be sending. It is capable of generating a recovery phrase. Make sure that it comes from a legit seller of hardware wallets to avoid losing your Bitcoin. There are instances where fake hardware wallets were able to steal the stored cryptocurrencies of the users.

Security threats to Bitcoin wallet

The most common security risks that can jeopardize Bitcoin wallets include:

> Malicious software malware that can steal your private keys by scanning the hard drive of your computer
> Digital exchange platforms that steal bitcoins by conducting "exit scams"
> A Trojan virus that encrypts your hard drive files, allowing the hacker to find the links to your Bitcoin wallet and see how much you own, then make a demand to send the fund in anonymous account in exchange for decrypting your hard drive. This modus is known as ransomware.
> Losing your phone, tablet, iPad, or laptop where you installed your wallet

Ways to protect your Bitcoin wallets

Just like the wallet in your pocket or purse, it is important to keep your Bitcoin wallet safe at all times.

> If possible, use cold storage options that do not require internet connectivity to make transactions.

- Be cautious and always double-check the emails or notifications you receive. There is a kind of scam known as "phishing" where a fake website of a wallet provider would send a message. Once you give authorization, it can wipe out all your bitcoins.
- Avoid checking unknown websites that may contain malware and compromise your funds if you are using a mobile or desktop Bitcoin wallet.
- Never give your private key to anyone or send it through messenger or email
- Do not entertain requests of unknown users who would ask for a BTC and promise to return more coins. They are scammers.

Key Point

Losing your private keys means loss of access to your Bitcoin address and bitcoins. According to researches, about 60% of Bitcoin addresses are now ghosts or their owners have lost their private keys.

Is there a physical Bitcoin?

Yes, there are physical coins that function as a bitcoin vault and a collector's item. They are preloaded with Bitcoin. The amount is fixed and the private key is protected by a tamper-evident seal. The most common are silver Bitcoin coins, but there are also golden or bronze coins. Each requires an upfront investment to own it.

You can also opt for physical coins that allow funding an amount of bitcoin to the address. These types of coins come with funding instructions. You can only spend them by breaking the protective hologram to retrieve the hidden private key. Once you redeem your coin, it will lose its digital value.

What is the real worth of physical bitcoins?

The value of physical bitcoins is often more than its actual worth because of their collectability and rarity when the minting of the range stops. Even without the Bitcoin value, the empty coins have their unique numismatic value. On eBay, the price for 125 unloaded Casascius coins is $4,995. A 2012 Casascius coin with 1 BTC value but was already peeled was bought by a private bidder for $1,999,99 on eBay.

The market of physical Bitcoin

The market is typically a niche for Bitcoin diehard enthusiasts and collectors who want physical coins for a series of collectibles, geek gifts, or conversation pieces. They are typically produced as limited series and when the last one was bought, they disappear from the market. The first physical Bitcoin coin was Bitbill. It came in the form of a credit card.

Some of the well-known physical bitcoins are:

- **Casascius** – Minted by Mike Caldwell in 2011, the Casascius coins came in different values such as 1 BTC brain coin, 0.5 BTC token, or 1,000 BTC gold-plated bar. The 25-Bitcoin denomination of Casascius coin is minted using brass material with gold electroplating.

   To cash in any of these Bitcoin coins, you need to remove the holographic sticker to get hold of the key to the wallet that contains the designated amount of bitcoins. This process is called "unpeeling."

   Unfortunately, Caldwell had to close his coin minting business in 2013 because he refused to register it at the federal level. The FinCEN or US Financial Crimes Enforcement Network classified his activity as "money transmitting." At the time of the closure, he already minted a total of 27,938 coins with different values.

CasasciusTracker reported that this coin is still worth a lot. Out of the total number, the active Casascius in circulation were 19,924 as of September 21, 2021. About 8,014 have been redeemed by their owners. Assuming that all the remaining coins have a 1 BTC value, it means that they are worth more than 851 million based on the current price of Bitcoin.

- **Titan Bitcoin** – The company offers a variety of coins from the priciest to the cheapest options. This is to allow clients to choose the option that matches their budget. The denominations range from 0.5 to 1 BTC.

  The most expensive is the Titan One Gold coin. It is loaded with 1 BTC and 1 troy ounce of 24K gold. The cheaper option is the 1-ounce .999 silver coin with 1 BTC which costs $729. There is also a 12 nickel-silver alloy Titan Tenth coin with 0.1 BTC and is priced $96 per piece.

- **Alitin Mint** – This Springfield, Missouri company minted two popular coins. The first one was the Adam Smith coin with 2

BTC load and the second was the Joan of Arc coin with 1 BTC. Both were commemorative 2-ounce pure silver coins designed by the renowned sculptor John Andelin.

Each variant has 600 minted coins. The Adam Smith coins are retailed for 2.92 BTC, while the Joan of Arc coins cost 1.45 BTC. Investors and collectors who bought this physical bitcoin in 2014 paid $378 per coin.

- **Cryptmint coins** – These .999 silver coins are sold for $99. They weigh 1 troy ounce with a diameter of 39 mm. Another option is the copper coins with a selling price of $42 apiece. There are 6 different QR back designs to choose from. They ship without preloaded bitcoin.

- **Ravenbit Satoshi coins** – Each Satoshi coin is 39mm in diameter and 3mm thick. Made of 85% copper, the front part of every coin has a person outline with binary codes that unlock the word 'Satoshi Nakamoto'. Each kit costs $25 and contains a coin, 2 security holograms, a display stand, and a pouch.

- **CoinedBit**s – They are novelty items without a Bitcoin value or physical wallet. Each collectible coin costs $14.99

for buyers in North America. For overseas buyers, the price is $19.99. They are made of pure brass with an 18K gold plating. Each coin has a 38mm diameter and weighs 1 ounce.

- **Antana coins** – These novelty coins are relatively affordable and created with names that are amusing. Every batch comes in a particular theme with a period of network statistic data. Some of the batch names were the "Transaction Malleability," "Goodbye Mt Gox", "Race for ROI", and "Pump and Dump". A complete set has 20 Antana bitcoins and is prized at 0.41 BTC, while individual coins sell for 0.02 BTC- 0.04 BTC.

- **Lealana coins** – Priced from 0.042 BTC-0.325 BTC are the unfunded gold-plated silver 1 BTC-Lealana coin. There is also a silver bitcoin set that contains 4 coins and is sold at 0.891 BTC.

Fun Fact
There are about 57 types of physical crypto coins. Most of them carry bitcoin value. This information came from Elias Ahonen's Encyclopedia of Physical Bitcoins and Crypto-currencies.

Is it legal to possess a physical Bitcoin?

Holding physical bitcoins is legal, provided that your location allows it. However, manufacturing or minting your own coins requires registration to ensure that your operation is not related to money transmission.

When buying physical coins in online marketplaces, make deals with legitimate sellers who will give you what you are paying for. Do your research diligently and have a ceiling of how much you can afford.

Key takeaways

- Bitcoin is the undisputed king of cryptocurrency, not because it is the pioneer virtual currency but because it has proven its worth.

- Satoshi Nakamoto's visionary and revolutionary concept of currency is now one of the valuable assets in the world.

- Bitcoin's blockchain technology has been copied and improved by modern creators who want to mimic or surpass the success of Bitcoin.

- The unique characteristics of Bitcoin that were once considered weaknesses are now its greatest strengths.

Point to Ponder

Should you buy Bitcoin or Gold?
In 2017, 1 bitcoin surpassed the price
of 1 troy ounce of gold.

Chapter 2

The Digital Gold Rush

"Bitcoin and its ilk are entertainment assets that provide 'psychic income."

Dennis Chookazian, Crypto analyst and futurist

Once an ambitious, futuristic project of pseudonymous Satoshi Yakamoto, Bitcoin proves itself to be more than that. It went beyond the skepticism and doubts, becoming the trailblazer of the future technology and giving virtual currencies a monetary role in the modern world.

Today, Bitcoin's network is growing stronger and has sparked the interest of new and big investors who want to diversify their wealth portfolio.

What's in store for Bitcoin now that it has established its mark in economic development?

Crypto analysts and experts believe that Bitcoin can be a strong instrument to resolve big global issues.

1. As a new form of investment, Bitcoin can utilize smart contracts and give investors easy exposure and access to stocks in foreign countries. This eliminates the need to find trusted brokers or intermediaries to sell the stocks.

2. As an instrument for money transfer or remittances of migrant workers. Transaction fees can be around 10 to 15% of the amount. With over $500 billion global remittances annually, it means that $50 billion or higher goes to the fees. Bitcoin can help reduce or eliminate the exorbitant fees.

3. As an enabler of functions of home electronics like televisions, refrigerators, washing machines, and so on. It works by sending a fraction of Bitcoin to the seller every month or week to make them run. It is a developing concept, but as I see it, everything is possible with Bitcoin.

Bitcoin is known for its ability to make people rich quickly. No other financial vehicles can match what Bitcoin has shown. It is also the fastest-growing asset in the world, where over 2% of the global population are now Bitcoin proud owners and still counting.

Not only that, more and more major players in various industries are showing their interest in cryptocurrency, in particular Bitcoin. Social Capital CEO Chamath Palihapitiya even made a fearless forecast that in the next 15 years, 1 bitcoin will be worth $1 million. If this happens, holding your investment for a while is a good decision. Your Bitcoin can make you an instant millionaire. But of course, it depends on how aggressive you are in accumulating bitcoins.

Did you know that?

Former child actor and entrepreneur Brock Pierce is the first person to get a crypto-based mortgage. He invested 3 million BTC to purchase a chapel in Amsterdam, The Netherlands.

Meet the world's Bitcoin billionaires and millionaires

Everyone who invests in Bitcoin wants to be a millionaire. Those who bought Bitcoin for under $10 when it was launched or less than $20,000 in the early part of 2018 earned huge profits after holding it for a time being. The sudden growth and demand of this cryptocurrency produced many Bitcoin millionaires and a handful of billionaires.

The Early Birds

These are people who bought Bitcoin during its early stage. Those who went all-in became billionaires, while others who were more conservative in their purchases became millionaires.

Cameron and Tyler Winklevoss

Many believed that former Olympic rowers and twin brothers Cameron and Tyler Winklevoss were the first bitcoin billionaires when the bitcoin price surged in 2017. They used the $65 million settlement from Facebook to buy bitcoins in 2012. After 5 years, their investment paid off, making them billionaires during the bull period.

The twins claimed to possess 1% of circulating bitcoins or about 100,000 coins that are worth $950 million. They also invested in other cryptocurrencies like Ethereum and various blockchain-related businesses. The twin's great interest in crypto prompted them to devise their own system of storing the private keys of their crypto assets. They eventually launched Gemini, the world's first regulated crypto exchange. The Winklevoss brothers also bought

Nifty Gateway, the auction platform for digital art.

Michael Saylor

Before his company decided to invest in Bitcoin, MicroStrategy CEO Michael Saylor was already investing in cryptocurrency. He made his fortune in investing but lost most of it during the dot.com bust. But instead of stopping, Saylor continued investing in Bitcoin and soon enough gained more than what he lost.

One time, Saylor tweeted that he was "hodling" 17,732 BTC and bought each coin at an average price of $9,882. His fascination with Bitcoin even led him to invest $1000 every second. He is among the top 100 BTC owners according to BitInfoCharts and on the 2021 Forbes' Billionaires List of crypto tycoons.

Matthew Roszak

Matthew Roszak became interested in Bitcoin way back 2011 and began buying to diversify his investment. After a decade, his crypto portfolio is already worth $1.5 billion. He also produced the first-ever documentary in the crypto industry- 'The Rise and Rise of Bitcoin."

This 48-year-old entrepreneur is the chairman and co-founder of the blockchain tech startup Bloq, which offers consultancy on projects that involve digital assets. Roszak also co-founded

Tally Capital, a cryptocurrency and blockchain-enabled technology investment firm with an impressive portfolio of major companies like Binance, Spacechain, Block. One, Blockstream, Spacechain, Orchid, Qtum, Tzero, Messari, and Civic.

Tim Draper

Tim Draper is a venture capitalist in Silicon Valley who purchased 29,656 bitcoins worth $18.7 million from the Silk Road black market stash that the U.S. Marshals seized in 2014. Apparently, each coin was worth $632 that time. Today, his bitcoins put him on the list of the crypto-rich people in Forbes Magazine.

He co-founded venture capital company Draper Fisher Jurvetson and has multiplied his worth by investing in cryptocurrencies, especially Bitcoin. Draper is also known for his VC investments in leading firms like Theranos and Tesla.

Barry Silvert

Barry Silbert is the founder-CEO of Digital Currency Group. This crypto conglomerate company invested in over 125 blockchain-related firms. His corporate portfolio includes Grayscale Investment, Genesis, and CoinDesk. Silvert's goal is to accelerate the global development of the financial system by establishing and supporting Bitcoin and other blockchain companies.

Michael Novogratz

When the crypto bull market happened in September 2017, Michael Novogratz claimed that he earned $250 million from his Bitcoin and Ethereum holdings. He purchased a private jet from the profits. After a year, he founded Galaxy Digital Holdings and invested $302 million to the company. His investment fund company trades, advises, and manages blockchain-related assets. It has a holding of 13,338 bitcoins which are valued at $122.5 million.

It is reported that 20% of Novogratz worth is in the form of digital assets and 30% of his fortune is tied to cryptocurrencies. He started investing around 2015. In 2017, he disclosed that he has a $500 million crypto fund, including $150 million from his vast fortune. He is known for being a prominent predictor of Bitcoin's market price movements.

Dan Morehead

Dan Morehead founded Pantera Capital, the first investment company that focuses on bitcoin. In 2018, it was one of the biggest institutional crypto holders. His company launched the first crypto fund in the United States when the trading price of bitcoin was only $65. When the crypto boom occurred in 2017, there was a report that the bitcoin fund of Pantera Capital managed to gain 24,000% for their investors. The company's portfolio investments include Shapeshift, Polychain Capital, Brave, and Bitstamp.

Why do institutional investors change their minds about Bitcoin?

For many years, the idea of Bitcoin investing is far from the minds of people behind large companies. They probably wondered why retail investors willingly embraced the volatility of this cryptocurrency and added it to their portfolios. Perhaps the thought of adding Bitcoin into their corporate reserves was not even entertained, considering their foremost requirement is stability and security of funds.

Then, pandemic happened and there was a Bitcoin frenzy. The taboo discussion about crypto investing became a crucial matter among big names in the financial industry. Suddenly, the gradual adoption of major companies in different industries has changed the landscape of cryptocurrency. Digital coins and tokens have been recognized as investable asset classes.

As of July 2021, the top publicly traded companies owning the largest Bitcoin reserve include the following in no particular order:

MicroStrategy

MicroStrategy opened the floodgates of institutional investment. This prominent cloud software company purchased Bitcoin for $425 million in August and September 2020, adopting it as a primary reserve asset. It continued buying Bitcoin until 2021 and is now holding a reserve asset of 105,085 BTC, which is worth more than $3.3 billion.

On the eve of New Year 2020, MicroStrategy sold its 10.9% share of Bitcoin to Morgan Stanley, a leading wealth management firm and global investment bank.

Quick Facts

Did you know that in 2013 MicroStrategy CEO Michael Saylor said that the days of Bitcoin were numbered?
But then he saw its potential returns and eventually chose it as his company's reserve asset over gold.

Tesla

Tesla has invested $1.50 billion in cryptocurrency according to its file in the SEC. CEO Based on its SEC filing, the company's purchase reflected its updated investment policy to maximize returns and diversify cash on hand.

Tesla invested in various alternative reserve assets such as digital assets (crypto), gold exchange-traded funds, gold bullions, and other future-specified assets. During the first quarter of 2021, Tesla sold 10% of its holdings to prove Bitcoin's liquidity as an option to cash. At present, it owns 42,902 BTC worth $1.37 billion.

Quick Facts

Elon Musk is a known holder of Bitcoin, so it seems natural that his electric vehicle manufacturing company would also adopt Bitcoin.

Square Inc.

When payments company Square Inc. invested $50 million to buy Bitcoin, it further lit the interest of institutional players to look at cryptocurrency with bigger interest. During the

4th Quarter of 2020, the company reported an additional $170 million Bitcoin investment in its earnings statement.

In March 2021, Square Inc. reaffirmed its commitment to holding its Bitcoin in a long-term period by revealing a reserve of 8,207 BTCs worth $255 million. The company has no future plan to buy more Bitcoin but is making efforts to leverage its ecosystem by investing a $5 million fund for cryptocurrency education. Moreover, it showed its support to Bitcoin when it issued a white paper that defended cryptocurrency's impact on the environment.

In July 2021, Square Inc. announced that they would create a hardware wallet for Bitcoin.

Quick Facts

CEO Jack Dorsey is a Bitcoin advocate who even has his own Bitcoin node.

Galaxy Digital Holdings

With over 16,640 BTC, Galaxy Digital Holdings is one of the biggest institutional holders that are working directly with the crypto industry. This crypto-focused merchant institution has partnered with BlockFi and Block. one. Its current Bitcoin holdings are worth more than $522 million.

Galaxy Digital Holdings founder Michael Novogratz is also an active Bitcoin advocate. When the stimulus measures to mitigate the effects of the COVID-19 pandemic were announced in April 202, he noted the strong interest of many firms in cryptocurrencies. He called the escalated attention as the 'Bitcoin moment'.

Coinbase Global Inc.

Crypto exchange Coinbase is one of the renowned firms that went public in April 2021. This move was considered a significant landmark in the cryptocurrency industry. Before its Nasdaq listing decision, Coinbase announced in February 2021 that its Bitcoin holding was around $230 million. By July 2021, the value of its 4,482 BTC went down to $143 million.

Voyager DigitalLTD

According to bitcoin treasuries.org, this renowned crypto brokerage firm has about 12,260 BTC worth $390 million. Voyager Digital operates by providing a one-stop digital trading shop that reported $60.4 million quarterly revenue in May 2021. It was 16 times bigger compared to the previous quarter.

Marathon Digital Holdings Inc.

Marathon Digital is a Bitcoin mining company with around 5,784 BTC worth $184 million in its treasury. It was established to become the 'biggest North America's Bitcoin mining firm' with the least energy expenses. Before it pivoted to crypto mining, Marathon Digital was a patent-holding company.

At the beginning of 2021, it added $200 million capital and ended January by purchasing $150 million worth of Bitcoin. Its long-term goal is to round up more than 103,000 Bitcoin miners to churn out around 50 to 60 BTC every day or an average of 1500 to 1800 BTC per month. As of June 2021, Marathon Digital was generating a monthly output of 265.6 BTC.

Hut 8 Mining Corp

With 3,522 BTC worth $112 million, Hut 8 is one of the major companies on the list. According to its SEC filing document, this Canadian-based crypto mining company "aims to grow the number and value of its bitcoin holdings to increase the shareholders' value." Also included is the explanation that it will be leveraging its held and self-mined Bitcoin reserve by partnering with the leading digital asset brokerages.

Hut 8 aims to mine 5,000 BTC by the year-end. It has invested in new crypto mining equipment and is riding on the favorable geopolitical landscape due to China's crackdown that reduced the difficulty of mining Bitcoin.

Bitcoin Group SE

Bitcoin Group SE is a venture capital company that is based in Germany. It is now holding around 3,947 BTCs which are worth $126 million based at the current price.

In October 2020, its Futurum bank and crypto exchange Bitcoin.de. have merged to become the first crypto bank in Germany. It came through after the German parliament allowed traditional banks to store and sell cryptocurrencies. It gave them a big opportunity to introduce the high returns and safety features of Bitcoin and other crypto to their institutional investors.

Riot Blockchain, Inc.

This US-based crypto mining company has 2,243 BTC holdings worth around $71 million. Riot Blockchain Inc. bought a Bitcoin mining facility for $650 million in Rockdale Texas in April 2021.

Its purchase of this 1-gigabyte facility was described in the crypto industry as an 'event of transformation'. It made the company North America's biggest publicly traded Bitcoin mining and hosting entity in terms of total developed capacity

Cool Fact

The U.S. United Wholesale Mortgage announced that they will be accepting Bitcoin and other cryptos as a mortgage payment.

The institutional investing landscape by waves

During the last two years before the pandemic, there was a growing interest and excitement about bitcoin among institutional investors. Bitcoin is seen by most of them as a hedge fund again inflation.

March 2020: The first wave

The sudden increase in the numbers of bitcoin that big investors bought was seen during the middle part of March 2020. Large companies and investors were reportedly buying a minimum of 1000 bitcoin. This phenomenon was described by industry experts as a move to secure hedge funds. Investing over $30 million in individual purchases means that the wealthiest and most powerful entities were busy safeguarding their holdings against potential risks.

Since crypto is deregulated and is not affected by economic downtrends, the money of the institutions is intact and secure. However, it was not surprising because many family-owned firms, hedge funds, and investment funds were already buying bitcoin. It was only highlighted when the CEOs of major companies and institutions became very vocal about their plans and decisions.

In April 2021, Coinbase confirmed that indeed, the big buyers were institutional investors. In its 1st quarter report, this leading crypto platform revealed that $215 billion out of its $335 billion in trades were made by the leading institutions and corporations.

The buying spree accelerated in October, then reached its peak in the early part of February 2021 when the price of 1 bitcoin reached

$33,000. The last high-water mark was during the Bitcoin bubble in 2017 when bitcoin's price reached $20,000.

The first wave ended at the end of the month. The data revealed that many big investors were busy selling their bitcoins and earning huge profits. They believed that the price won't go beyond $33,000, so they sold their investment.

May 2021: The current wave

Since this May, the escalating growth of big investors rebuying bitcoins has become significant. There is no indication of slowing down, yet. It seems that Bitcoin has found its long-term position in the institutional portfolios.

Perhaps, one of the reasons for this stronger interest in this volatile crypto asset was due to the phenomenal price surge of $64,486 per BTC on April 14, 2021. Those who sold their coins in February were surprised by the development. And what made bitcoin more attractive during that period was its display of price durability.

In May 2021, bitcoin was trading more than $55,000. On May 11, it was fetching $56,800 then scaled down to $35,000 at the end of the month. The sudden change was due to the growing criticism regarding the environmental impact of bitcoin. But for institutional and big investors, this lull was an opportunity to jump back in their bitcoin buying spree.

They saw the April price of bitcoin as a good indicator of its strong market position, making them more confident to invest more. The mid-May price of $35,000 attracted them back. In addition, while the sharp and fast fall of bitcoin price in May was felt in the industry, many saw that bitcoin can survive amidst the system's loss of leverage. It has found its own leverage level that prompted the investors to trust its power of stability and sustainability. It triggered this current wave.

> ### Did you know that?
>
> *The most valuable hard drive happened to be the one that British James Howells accidentally threw in 2013?*
> *It contained over 75,000 BTCs which is worth $2.25 billion or more.*

Bitcoin price in institutional investment

Bitcoin's power to stay on top of the crypto industry lies in its proprietary blockchain data and its pricing durability. Institutional investors are more than willing to spend more than

$36,000 for one BTC. As of September 2021, 1 BTC is priced at $43,000. They keep buying and haven't sold their holdings yet.

It is also interesting to note that these institutional investors can leverage their power in the crypto market, with their valuation influencing the price of Bitcoin. Also, with the largest financial firms and banks planning or offering access to bitcoins and other cryptocurrencies to their existing big clients, acceleration of institutional buying would be a common scenario for a long time.

Institutional investors consider bitcoin as digital gold, like precious metals to secure their wealth. They buy and hold bitcoin and altcoins to hedge their investment against constant inflation as well as diversify their financial portfolio. Also, compared to gold and other precious metals, bitcoin's evolving technology promises bigger growth potential. The technological innovations boost its current value and attractiveness to investors.

As of August 2021, Buy Bitcoin Worldwide data revealed that institutional investors are holding around $70 billion worth of Bitcoin or an equivalent of 1,476,568 BTC. This number is 7.85% of the 18,797,968 circulating supply of bitcoin in the market.

The gold rush is digital

The craze around Bitcoin becomes stronger as it reaches more than a decade of existence in the digital realm. Its decentralized approach is a big come-on for techie-driven economists, investors, and traders. It was like the 1848 gold rush where the elite group in the society wanted the asset in their possession, as gold represents power, fame, and status symbol.

Bitcoin is a game-changer, creating an unprecedented path that no other digital currency has done. While the journey to the top was tough, it displayed resilience and flexibility to be recognized in the digital world.

Whether you love or hate cryptocurrency, it is here and part of the modern world. The future is still unknown but there are expert predictions that crypto, especially Bitcoin, would continue shaping the virtual realm and go mainstream. By allowing users to buy, sell, exchange, or hold money without government or central bank authority oversight, crypto acts as the cutting edge of finance.

Ways organized crime syndicates exploit the digital gold rush

Aside from the traders and investors, there are groups of people or individuals who are leveraging the digital gold rush to accomplish their illicit activities. They conceal their organized crimes behind the anonymity feature of cryptocurrencies. In Latin America, unscrupulous people use Bitcoin in the following organized crimes:

- **Money Laundering** – Gangs are hiding behind the anonymous feature of cryptocurrencies.

  - The Unidad de Inteligencia Financiera (UIF) of Mexico is running after illegal crypto exchanges where money laundering is rampant.

➢ In Rio de Janeiro, 12 people were arrested and charged with laundering extorted money from local businesses. The Civil Police said that they were using Bitcoin to hide their operations. They bought small amounts of bitcoins and stored them in different anonymous digital wallets.

➢ Venezuela is also raising questions about how the cash machines in Caracas can be utilized for illicit money laundering. According to the report of the Drug Enforcement Administration, anyone can deposit cash into these ATMs to buy Bitcoin. They believe that once the fiat currency is in the digital form, it would be easy to hide where it originated, allowing transfer from one user to another anywhere in the world.

- **Ransomware Extortion** – It refers to the data hostage operation of criminals who typically ask crypto payments as ransom. This extortion activity usually locks the target's computer system or steals its corporate data.

One notable victim of a ransomware attack was JBS, the Brazilian meat processing firm that is supplying 1/5 of beef consumption in the United States. It paid the group "REvil" a ransom of $11 million worth of bitcoins.

- **Kidnapping** – Another syndicated crime where Bitcoin is being used as ransom payment is kidnapping. In Tia Juana Venezuela, the kidnapped victim Gustavo Torres Gonzales was murdered when his family did give the full amount of Bitcoin to the kidnappers. Another story of kidnapping happened in Argentina, where a merchant was finally released after 5 days of being held captive when the family paid the demanded ransom in Bitcoin.

- **Ciberburreros (Cyber mules)** – They are young people used by the criminal syndicates to purchase small volumes of crypto simultaneously. Since smaller transactions are not suspicious, the group behind them would be accumulating large holdings of digital currencies to use in criminal activities including money laundering. The pattern of their activities mimics the way the Sinaloa Cartel moved drugs in the U.S.

Getting onboard to the digital gold rush

It appears that 2021 is becoming the year of Bitcoin, making the pioneer cryptocurrency live up to being the 'digital gold.' While the world is battling the COVID-19 pandemic threats, Bitcoin has become an attractive cushion against inflation.

Goldman Sachs and Paul Tudor Jones recognized and endorsed it as digital gold, while the likes of MicroStrategy, Grayscale, and MassMutual welcomed it as part of their investment portfolio. PayPal also delved into the crypto world by adding Bitcoin and selected altcoins to its services.

Should you join the Bitcoin feeding frenzy?

The Bitcoin market is volatile. It started 2021 on a strong and high note and more bitcoins are changing hands. These are signs of a liquid, active, and healthy crypto market. Traders and holders of BTC who panicked with sudden dips of its market value sold their coins to many Bitcoin 'whales'. These investors have over 1,000 bitcoins in their possession and are always on the lookout for retail investors who are selling their crypto out of fear that the price crash would continue.

But a lot of institutional investors, crypto-analysts, and industry specialists are predicting a sunny outlook for this cryptocurrency over the next year or beyond. One leaked report coming from a senior analyst of Citibank revealed that Bitcoin has a high potential to reach another all-time high in December 2021 with a projected value of $318,000. If this happens, then Bitcoin is set to become the "gold of the 21st century."

Other predictions include:

> StormGain CEO Alex Althausen predicted that Bitcoin's market price would hit $100,000 by the end of the year.

> JP Morgan strategists believed that once Bitcoin beats its volatility, it could replace gold as the preferred safe-haven asset and achieve a long-term value of $146,000 per coin.

> Guggenheim's predicts that the price of Bitcoin would soar at $400,000.

Another interesting set of Bitcoin predictions for 2022 came from the Chief Economist Philip Gradwell of Chainalysis. He advised investors, in particular institutional sectors, to watch out for the following factors when advancing their investing strategies:

- Bitcoin will sustain its price floor of $36,000 until the summer of 2022.

- Bitcoin will continue its domination among large investors, followed by Ethereum.

- The next batch of Bitcoin investors would want the risks and flaws in the system resolved. Expect major activities in the system and crypto industry to elevate the status of Bitcoin and make it comparable with the gold-standard characteristics of conventional investment instruments.

- The liquidity of Bitcoin will surge as institutional investors buy and sell their crypto in shorter terms. In essence, more liquidity means a more mature Bitcoin market.

- As large investors aim for ESG investing or socially responsible investing, there would be actions and reforms in the crypto industry to reduce the environmental impact of their mining activities. To boost the confidence of investors in virtual currencies, Bitcoin Mining Council and other groups would actively address the ESG (Environmental, Social, and Governance) issues.

- There would be a stronger pursuit for regulations and perimeter settings.

- Skeptics and doubters who are afraid of catastrophic collapse will significantly decrease.

Trivia

When the IRS won the case against Coinbase, the exchange company was required to submit the list of 14,000 users with more than $20,000 cost of transactions between 2013 and 2015.

List of countries that say "Yay" and "Nay" on Bitcoin

After its 2009 debut, Bitcoin remains a hot subject of debate among regulators, enforcement agencies, and tax authorities. Until today, there is no single international law that can regulate the peer-to-peer transactions of Bitcoin.

However, the issue and question of its legality depends on the location and the activities of users. Some countries have enacted regulatory oversight that indirectly allows its legal use, while others prefer to wait-and-see what will be the consensus of the majority.

12 Countries that show to Bitcoin

El Salvador

El Salvador formally adopted bitcoin as a legal tender when President Nayib Bukele signed the "Bitcoin Law" on June 8, 2021. Bitcoin officially joined the US dollar as El Salvador's legal tender on September 7, 2021. This historical decision made them the first-ever country to completely legalize the status of Bitcoin, recognizing its economic value.

- ✓ The Salvatorian government also purchased 400 bitcoins worth $21 million as a buffer fund.

- ✓ Chivo wallet, a Bitcoin wallet that is officially sponsored by the government has been downloaded by almost 46% of the population or about 3 million people one month after the law became effective on September 21, 2021.

The United States

Generally, there is a positive response toward Bitcoin in the United States. More and more prominent retail companies are welcoming bitcoin payment including Microsoft, Subway, and Dish Network (DISH). In addition, Bitcoin has successfully made its way to the derivatives market which adds to its sense of legitimacy.

- • Bitcoin is categorized Bitcoin as a money services business (MSB) by the U.S. Department of Treasury and not a currency. It means that all payment processors and exchanges that conduct business with Bitcoin should register, report, and keep records of the transactions as mandated by the bank Secrecy Act.

- The Treasury's FinCEN or Financial Crimes Enforcement Network has been issuing guidance about this cryptocurrency since 2013.

- The Internal Revenue Service (IRS) has put Bitcoin under the property for taxation purposes category, in particular federal income tax.

- The Securities and Exchange Commission (SEC) considers Bitcoin as a security asset.

- The Commodity Futures Trading Commission (CFTC) sees it as a commodity.

The European Union

When the European Court of Justice (ECJ) issued a ruling on October 22, 2015, that the buy and sell of cryptocurrencies is a form of supply of services, it exempted Bitcoin and other digital currencies from paying value-added tax (VAT) in all member states.

Also, some of the EU countries are making bitcoin stances in their own jurisdictions.

- ✓ The United Kingdom's Financial Conduct Authority (FCA) is pro-bitcoin and wants to have a supportive regulatory environment on this cryptocurrency. Bitcoin is also placed under some tax regulations.

- ✓ Belgium's Federal Public Service Finance gave Bitcoin a VAT-exempt status.

- ✓ Finland's Central Board of Taxes (CBT) has classified Bitcoin as a financial service to exempt it from VAT. It is treated as a form of commodity rather than a currency.

- ✓ Bulgaria's National Revenue Agency (NRA) has included Bitcoin in its tax laws.

- ✓ Cyprus has no regulations over Bitcoin, allowing its operations in the country.

- ✓ Germany considers Bitcoin legal but subjects it to taxes that cover exchanges, users, enterprises, or miners.

Australia

Bitcoin is considered an asset under capital gains tax purposes by the Australian Taxation Office (ATO). By classifying virtual currencies as legal properties, they are subject to capital gains tax.

- The government of the "Land Down Under" allows crypto exchanges to operate freely anywhere in the country, as long as the operators register their business with the AUSTRAC (Australian Transaction Reports and Analysis Centre). They should also meet the required AML/CTF obligations and conditions.

- For initial coin offerings (ICOs), the Australian Securities and Investments Commission (ASIC) issued strict regulatory requirements to protect investors.

- In 2019, authorities banned the crypto exchanges that offer privacy coins or coins with built-in privacy features due to the speculations that they could be used by syndicated criminal elements.

Canada

With a friendly stance on bitcoin, Canada considers it as a commodity under the ruling of the Canada Revenue Agency (CRA). All Bitcoin transactions are considered barter and the generated income is viewed as business income. The taxable amount is dependent on whether the person is into investing or conducting a buy and sell business.

- ✓ In February 2021, the government approved the Bitcoin exchange-traded fund (ETF), making Canada the first one to give one.

- ✓ The bitcoin exchanges are under the money service business, placing them under the Anti-Money Laundering (AML) laws. This is to ensure that Bitcoin cannot be used as an instrument for money laundering acts of unscrupulous people.

- ✓ The Investment Industry Regulatory Organization of Canada (IIROC) and the Canadian Securities Administrators (CSA) compelled all crypto dealers and trading platforms to register under respective provincial regulators.

Japan

Japan has a progressive stance when it comes to regulating cryptocurrencies. Under the Payment Services Act, Japanese authorities recognize Bitcoin and other virtual currencies as legal property.

- All crypto exchanges should register with FSA (Financial Services Agency) and comply with the obligations of AML/CFT.

- The trading gains from crypto are considered as "miscellaneous income" and investors are taxed accordingly.

Singapore

In the island state of Singapore, cryptocurrencies are classified as property. All exchanges need to secure a license to operate from the Monetary Authority of Singapore (MAS) and follow the applicable regulations that are listed in the Payment Services Act (PSA).

- Singapore treats the gains of crypto companies as income and is subject to corresponding taxes.
- However, it does not tax long-term capital gains.

Mauritius

The country's Financial Services Commission considers Bitcoin and other cryptocurrencies as Digital Assets under the 2007 Financial Services Act. While virtual currencies are regulated, the authorities are still cautioning investors to be careful even though they are covered by the statutory compensation agreements protection.

Mexico

Since 2017, Bitcoin has been legal in the country. The plans to regulate this cryptocurrency as a Virtual Asset under FinTech Law are in progress.

Kyrgyzstan

Under the Kyrgyz Republic laws, Bitcoin is a commodity and not a currency or security. It is legal to mine, buy, sell, or trade this crypto on its local commodity exchanges. However, using bitcoin as a currency to settle domestic settlements is still prohibited.

Uzbekistan

This crypto-friendly territory has legalized crypto-trading and makes it tax-exempt by virtue of a decree that was signed on September 2, 2018.

Switzerland

All forms of Bitcoin businesses in this country are subject to the laws against money laundering. In some cases, Bitcoin entrepreneurs need to obtain a banking license before they can conduct their ventures. As of June 2021, there are about 100 Exchange Traded Products (ETP) in the country.

10 Countries that are UNFRIENDLY to Bitcoin

China

First on the list is China. The People's Bank of China (PBOC) has banned all Bitcoin transactions and crypto exchanges in the country. This is due to the no-approval transaction method that Bitcoin offers to users.

- All banks, payment processors, and other financial institutions are prohibited to deal or transact using Bitcoin.

- It has a continuing order to crack down on any crypto mining activities, forcing firms that are engaged in this activity to relocate or close their operations.

- In 2017, Binance which was launched in China relocated to the Cayman Islands when the authorities began their crackdown on cryptocurrency regulations.

Bolivia

There is an absolute ban on any use of Bitcoin and altcoins in the country according to El Banco Central de Bolivia.

Ecuador

In a national assembly, the majority of people voted against the use of cryptocurrencies including Bitcoin in the country.

Egypt

A religious decree that classified all Bitcoin commercial transactions as 'Haram" (prohibited under the laws of Islam) was issued by the Islamic legislator Egypt's Dar al-lfta.

Russia

While Russia does not have a standing regulation about Bitcoin, using it to pay for goods and services is considered illegal.

Vietnam
The government of Vietnam as well as the state bank stand on their decisions that Bitcoin cannot be used as a legitimate form of payment.

Saudi Arabia

All financial institutions in the country are warned by the Saudi Central Bank (SAMA) not to use Bitcoin because of its high-risk nature.

Qatar

Cryptocurrencies are prohibited in the Qatar Financial Centre and all banks cannot trade Bitcoin because of the threats involving hacks and financial crimes.

Bangladesh

All financial institutions in the country are prohibited to conduct any form of Bitcoin transactions. The Bangladesh Bank issued a statement in September 2014 that 'anyone caught using crypto would be charged and imprisoned under its anti-money laundering laws.'

Nepal

There is an absolute ban on any kind of cryptocurrency in this country.

> **Key Points**
>
> *In the context of Bitcoin adoption, the 3 metrics must be present:*
> - *Number and presence of merchants that accept Bitcoin as payment.*
> - *Size of the population relative to Bitcoin activities.*
> - *Number and location of Bitcoin ATMs.*

Bitcoin Hotspots: Cities in the world that adopted Bitcoin

San Francisco (USA)

As the tech capital of the United States, it is expected to be part of the list since it is home to two prominent crypto trading platforms – Kraken and Coinbase. There are 65 Bitcoin ATMs in the city and 473 in the Bay Area.

Merchants and business establishments in this major US city accept bitcoins as payment for goods and services rendered.

Vancouver (Canada)

Did you know that the first Bitcoin ATM in the world was placed at Waves Coffee House in downtown Vancouver on October 29, 2013? The city was also the home of the defunct crypto exchange QuadrigaCX, which became controversial when it lost the clients' fund amounting to $180 million after the news of the alleged death of the founder was released to the public.

At present, the Bitcoin community in the whole of Canada is growing stronger. People can buy Bitcoin from 221 locations in the country with over 50 merchants accepting it as payment.

New York (USA)

Known as the tech and financial hub of over 8.4 million people, this city is the major location of crypto startups and crypto-media firms like CoinDesk, CoinTelegraph, and Decrypt. Anyone can use their bitcoin in the metro area when paying merchants and crypto traders.

In Lower Manhattan, there is a Bitcoin Store and in Morningside Heights, CryptoART is a to-go place for crypto enthusiasts. New York is also the venue of Consensus, which is one of the crypto industry's biggest annual events.

Amsterdam (Netherlands)

Amsterdam is where Bitfury, the mining hardware maker is located. It is also home to the European HQ of BitPay, one of the leading payment service providers. Placed in the city's strategic locations are half a dozen ATMs where you use to buy or sell bitcoins.

Tel Aviv (Israel)

Tel Aviv is one of the best cities for crypto startups. It has 7 Bitcoin ATMs and 19 merchants who accept Bitcoin payments across the metro. Tel Aviv is also home to the 4,000-member Israel Bitcoin Meetup Group which is one of the most active in the crypto world.

Portsmouth, New Hampshire (USA)

Known as the "Bitcoin village", this tiny coastal city has a large crypto community. There are 21 Bitcoin ATMs as well as tellers in the city and nearby areas. Portsmouth's downtown section is home to the Free State Bitcoin Shoppe, Seacoast Repertory Theater, and other crypto-friendly businesses.

Ljubljana (Slovenia)

It is the biggest city and capital of Slovenia with about 200 merchants accepting bitcoin payments and 11 ATMs where anyone can use for easy selling or buying of cryptocurrency. Bitstamp, the well-known Bitcoin exchange was founded by Slovenians who eventually moved their operations to London and Luxembourg.

Miami, Florida (USA)

This major city of the United States is actively seeking blockchain businesses to invest in their area. It has 651 Bitcoin ATMs and tellers as well as 4 dozen merchants who accept crypto payment.

The city government through Mayor Francis Suarez is proposing to integrate bitcoin in their transactions such as allowing the residents to pay taxes and fees using this cryptocurrency and exploring the possibility of paying the salary of government employees in Bitcoin. It was the venue of Miami Bitcoin Conference, the oldest and biggest crypto convention.

London (United Kingdom)

With over 8.9 million people, London has 50 Bitcoin ATMs across the city and merchants accepting Bitcoin as payment for purchases of goods and services. Coinfloor, the pioneer Bitcoin exchange in the United Kingdom has its HQ in this city. People embrace crypto as part of their daily transactions with dozens of Meetup groups that support Bitcoin and altcoins.

El Zonte (El Salvador)

El Zonte is a fishing and surfing village with 3,000 people. It has been using Bitcoin since 2019 when California surfer Mike Peterson who was doing charity work in the area received more than $100,000 donation from an anonymous American in one condition- the amount paid in bitcoins would be used to establish a local sustainable Bitcoin ecosystem. This unknown donor became rich because of crypto trading and wanted to show the world that Bitcoin can positively change the society's way of living.

The initiative was dubbed Bitcoin Beach where residents use an app payment system for crypto exchange. They initially received a certain amount to use for routine activities like paying utility bills, buying goods, and other daily transactions. The experiment was successful and has become the inspiration of President Nayib Bukele to push the law adopting Bitcoin as legal tender. In 2020, El Zonte received a Bitcoin ATM from the government.

Cool Fact

El Salvador President Nayib Bukele is a millennial business-politician who describes himself as the "world's coolest dictator," and a Silicon Valley-like

Key takeaways

- The impressive rate of Bitcoin adoption within the span of 10 years is a clear and strong indication that cryptocurrencies are already part of society's economic and financial sectors.

- Bitcoin has changed the landscape of the global investment sector, attracting major and prominent institutional investors to explore its unique features and benefits.

- The transformation of Bitcoin from a highly-speculative investment instrument to a trusted portfolio stablemate is being considered by the governments that are still figuring out how to regulate this asset class.

- Bitcoin has created a list of millionaires and billionaires across the world, attracting more retail investors to invest in Bitcoin and wait for the next digital gold rush.

- More and more countries are becoming "friendlier" to Bitcoin.

Point to Ponder

Want to jump into Bitcoin investing?
Learn more in the next chapter.

Chapter 3

Is Cryptocurrency Investing for You?

"In cryptocurrency investment, long-term thinkers are less stressed."
– Olawale Daniel-

In Bitcoin investing, anyone who dares becomes filthy wealthy or loses his money. If you're the type of investor who worries about losing money or the myriad of risks that come with the nature of crypto, this investing in Bitcoin is not for you. It is for investors who have strong risk tolerance and are not afraid to fail at the beginning of their investment journey.

In a nutshell, cryptocurrency is in the category of "high risk, high reward" investment. The main appeal of crypto investing lies in the potential of amassing huge profits that can make you an overnight millionaire. But what if you wake up one morning and find out that your crypto coin has lost its value because of the loss of support and adoption from major investors?

Reality bites, but it is how the world of crypto operates- volatile, proactive, highly speculative, and full of risks.

To be successful in Bitcoin and crypto investing, there are 3 things you need to do:

1. Expect that crypto investing is like a roller coaster ride, so plan and prepare your strategies.
2. Start with small sums to buy crypto or fractional shares of investment until such time that you are more skillful and confident.
3. Track down the performance of your crypto investment so you will know when to sell it.

The fundamentals of cryptocurrency investing

As Bitcoin and other cryptocurrencies go mainstream, it becomes impossible for investors to ignore the lure of investing in virtual currencies. Many are considering buying Bitcoin or altcoins to add to their financial portfolio, seeing how these digital currencies are not affected by economic and political events that can crash the stocks and the value of fiat currencies.

But first, you need to learn the basics. You cannot just buy a cryptocurrency and then sell it when you want. You need to plan, prepare, and apply your knowledge with diligence.

Get familiar with cryptocurrency

Cryptocurrency or crypto is a digital currency that is created through encryption technology. It takes a virtual form of coin or token, which is intangible in nature. The unique encryption algorithms of crypto make it both a currency for online transactions and a virtual accounting system.

It is designed to be decentralized and cannot be controlled or manipulated by anyone, even the government. Compared to conventional currencies, cryptocurrency does not possess the fundamental tenets like being a medium of exchange, store of value, or unit of measurement.

The term 'crypto' in cryptocurrency refers to the complex cryptography that is used to mine or create every single coin. Bitcoin is produced by the mining process, where 'miners' solve complicated mathematical problems. On the other hand, other cryptocurrencies are generated as code by professional teams that build proprietary mechanisms for issuance.

Blockchain: The heart and soul of crypto

Cryptocurrency exists in the virtual sphere and is powered by **blockchain**, the core technology with extremely strong cryptography that secures all transactions. It has its own mechanism that operates without any human intervention, storing information in blocks and chaining them together in chronological order.

Technically, a blockchain is a database that collects and stores data electronically in groups or blocks. This innovative technology enables users to collectively retain control over their own funds and deal with each other without intermediaries like a bank, government, or third party. The peer-to-peer transactions are verified, time-stamped, and recorded by the computer networks of the blockchain system.

And because it is decentralized, blockchain is immutable. It means that every information that users input into the system is irreversible and permanently recorded. Access to view the transactions is possible but not the confidential details of the users.

How does blockchain work?

For example, Mr. A wants to buy a bitcoin.

- The purchase and sale transaction is entered in the public digital ledger (blockchain) and then transmitted to the nodes (network of high-end, powerful computers) across the world.

- The network of nodes will individually assess and confirm the transaction with the help of computer algorithms. This process of solving equations is called "proof of work."

- Once the transaction is cryptographically confirmed as legitimate, it will be added to the block in the ledger.

- The new block will be chained to other blocks to create a permanent history of all transactions.

Mr. A's transaction is complete.

Trivia

The concept of blockchain was initially outlined by researchers
Stuart Haber and W.Scott Stornetta in 1991, but the real-world
application only happened in January 2009 when Bitcoin
was launched in public.

The Cryptocurrencies: Bitcoin and Altcoins

The crypto variants are mostly forks of Bitcoin and the rest were developed from scratch. In terms of types of cryptocurrencies, there are two broad types:

1. Bitcoin

Blockchain-based Bitcoin is the first decentralized cryptocurrency and the most successful. It sends users transactions over its proprietary blockchain and utilizes public-key cryptography for verifying, signing, and recording them. It was introduced to the world on January 3, 2009, by the anonymous programmer Satoshi Nakamoto. Until today, the persona behind Nakamoto is still a big mystery.

Bitcoin's network is designed to stop developing new coins when the 21-million cap is achieved. As of this time, the total circulation is over $18 million. This limited supply is the primary reason that drives Bitcoin's market price.

One bitcoin is equivalent to 100,000,000 satoshis. A single bitcoin can be divided up to 8 decimal places, giving investors an option to buy fractions for a more affordable price rather than paying more than $56,000 for a single bitcoin.

How does it operate?

Users of bitcoin send or receive coins by inputting the public-key data that is connected to their electronic wallet. There is a fee to every transaction and it is used to incentivize the miners or the network of people that verify the transaction. The miner who successfully adds the transaction to a fresh block gets the reward. The higher the transaction fee, the faster it will be processed by the miners since it operates on a first-price auction system.

The block rewards in the Bitcoin system decrease over time. At present (2021), the reward for mining new blocks is 6.25 bitcoins. For every 210,000 mined blocks (around a 4-year period), the reward is halved. The next halving of bitcoin will be in 2024, where the block reward will be dropping to 3.124 bitcoins for every block.

Trivia

Bitcoin (with uppercase "B") refers to the peer-to-peer decentralized system while the native cryptocurrency is called bitcoin (with lower case "b").

2. Altcoins

Altcoins or alternate versions of bitcoins are cryptocurrencies other than bitcoins.

They represent almost 60% of circulating more than 12,000 cryptocurrencies in the market as of October 2021. The price movements of altcoins usually copy the trajectory and trading signals of Bitcoin.

In the context of market capitalization, the largest altcoins are the Ethereum and Binance Coins. At present, there are more than 5,000 circulating altcoins in the world.

Altcoins are divided according to their consensus mechanisms and functionalities.

- Mining-based – These altcoins are produced by mining using Proof-of-Work (PoW). This method refers to the process where new coins are created by solving difficult equations or problems. Some examples are Litecoin, Zcash, and Monero.

  The alternative to this type of altcoins is the pre-mined coins. They are cryptocurrencies that are listed in the market before their distribution. Ripple's XRP is a good example.

- Stablecoins – These crypto are created to reduce the volatile nature of coins. They work by anchoring the value of the altcoin to the basket of financial products like fiat currencies, other types of crypto, or precious metals like gold or silver. The basket of goods serves as a reserve fund to redeem the crypto holders of their loss when the coin faces problems or fails to deliver the promise. Examples of stablecoins include MakerDAO, and USDC, and Facebook-backed Diem.

- Tokens – There are two kinds of token-utility and security. Utility tokens can be used to purchase services within the network, redeem rewards, or pay network fees. Filecoin is an example of this type of token.

  Security tokens are typically offered to potential investors via ICOs or initial coin offerings. They possess digital provenance and promise equity to the owners. Dividends are paid to the holders regularly. The price of these tokens appreciates over time.

- Meme coins – They are inspired by a joke on other crypto and gained popularity when famous crypto retail investors and personalities used the power of social media platforms to promote them. Dogecoin, for instance, experienced a 91% growth surge within 24-hours when Elon Musk of Tesla shared photos of his Shiba Inu puppy on Twitter.

Is cryptocurrency investing worth a try?

Crypto investing is a highly lucrative venture if you have a strong risk tolerance and willing to wait until the timing is right. The value of cryptocurrencies goes up because of speculations or when new investors are willing to pay more than the price the sellers set.

In order to profit from your investment, you need to wait for the demand to be strong and people want to own your coins no matter what the stake is. For Bitcoin buying and selling purposes, you need to register in a trusted crypto exchange.

For long-term investment goals, Bitcoin and Ethereum are two cryptocurrencies that are made for this purpose. They operate on the concept that if you invest now, you will gain incredible financial rewards in the future. The window of time is longer, but your ROI will give you financial freedom. This has happened to early investors of Bitcoin, who held their coins for a time being and sold them for huge profits.

Is it a wise investment?

The Bitcoin network is now valued at over $100 billion and there's no stopping its dominant role in the virtual world. As a pioneering crypto coin, Bitcoin's resilience has been established in its decade-plus existence. Its trailblazing ability has opened doors of possibilities and opportunities for traders, investors, and retailers across the globe.

Once regarded as the "money of the future", it is now accepted as payment for retail and trade transactions. For that reason alone, Bitcoin has proven its worth and power to penetrate the traditional market. Moreover, its popularity gave birth to the emergence of other cryptocurrencies or altcoins.

As an instrument of investment, cryptocurrency is highly speculative because of the absence of the underlying intrinsic value. Investors typically look into the intrinsic value of an asset or financial instrument to gauge if it is worth a try. It also them understand if the cost of getting it is overvalued or undervalued as compared to the asset's market value.

Cryptocurrency does not have an underlying value. It does not track the value of a natural resource or the growth potential of companies. Its value lies on users' and investors' trust and is not pegged on gold, metals, or fiat currency. In a nutshell, the return of your investment is determined by the people who are willing to pay more for your crypto coin in the future.

Bitcoin has established itself as a wise investment, creating a list of self-made millionaires and billionaires after betting for the power of crypto. But then, not all investors had the same fate. The dot.com era has become a dreaded part of the crypto history when investors lost so much when some crypto coins failed to deliver their promises. Hence, the importance of doing due diligence and not investing what you cannot afford to lose. Like any speculative game of chance or investment, crypto investing is either about winning big or losing big.

Is cryptocurrency safe?

In the world of investment, there is no such thing as 'safe'. It is a volatile, yet exciting world where risks and returns are the most important concepts. So, if you are asking me if crypto investing is safe, the answer is a resounding 'no', but it offers life-changing results.

The risks

- Vulnerability – One of the biggest concerns of potential investors is the cybersecurity issues that can wipe out their money in a blink of an eye. There were cases of security breaches and hackings in the past that cost investors millions of dollars. While exchange platforms are claiming strong security measures to protect their clients' investment, the threat is always there.

- Security of storage – Despite being virtual, cryptocurrencies need safe storage to protect them against theft or cyber hacking. This is where 'cold storage' becomes a better option than 'hot' or online storage, which essentially is leaving your money in crypto exchanges or brokers. Once your crypto coins are stolen, it is gone forever.

- Highly competitive arena – As cryptocurrencies become more mainstream and accepted as a mode of payment for various transactions, more and more crypto projects present themselves, attracting investors to support them. As competition becomes fierce, scams and fraudulent projects become more prevalent. If you have invested in a new crypto project, there is no guarantee that it will succeed.

- Price volatility – Warren Buffet once regarded the ecosystem of cryptocurrency as a bubble. The lack of inherent value is one big drawback, resulting in strong price volatility. History reveals that Bitcoin has suffered losing about 80% of its value when the market trends spiraled down, while Ethereum has lost almost 95% of its value in just a year.

- Decentralization – Cryptocurrency operates on its own, with the help of blockchain technology. No one controls, administers, evaluates, or supervises crypto operations. Until such time that the proprietary technology of crypto is recognized or adopted by the governments, the risk remains a strong concern.

The rewards

- Long-term store of value- Because of the mathematical algorithms cap, the value of cryptocurrency is not affected by inflation. In addition, because of its cryptographic nature, no authority can confiscate the coins or tokens unless the owner gives authorization. Its censorship-resistant and deflationary features make it extremely attractive to investors who worry about bank failures, inflationary events, and disasters.

- The potential of high returns– Undeniably, investors buy cryptocurrency because of the promise of big profits. If you do it right, you can say goodbye to your 9-to-5 job, and open your dream business, or live the life you want. In just one stroke of luck, your cryptocurrency can change your financial status.

- Confidentiality and transparency– For people who want to protect private financial information, crypto is the answer. This prevents becoming a victim of data breaches. In terms of transparency, crypto arms investors complete freedom and total control to conduct their transactions without any third party.

Why are you investing in crypto?

The most fundamental question to ask yourself is why you want to invest in cryptocurrency.

Your 'why or whys' would be your guideposts in your investing journey.

- *Why cryptocurrency when there are other investment vehicles that offer lesser risks and more stability?*

If you aim for **portfolio diversification**, cryptocurrency investment is a smart decision. Bitcoin is the all-time favorite, but there are many altcoins (alternative coins) that are performing well in the industry. However, before buying an altcoin, make sure that you have studied its profile to ensure that like Bitcoin, it guarantees stability during the test of time.

The increasing **cryptocurrency adoption by** financial giants in the industry is boosting the trust and confidence of investors. PayPal and Square make it easier for their users to buy and sell crypto coins and tokens. Tesla and other institutional investors bought Bitcoin and other types of cryptocurrencies to solidify and diversify their portfolios.

Blockchain is the future of technology. For more than a decade since Bitcoin was introduced, its underlying technology blockchain has been recognized in the industry as a game-changer that benefits other industries like healthcare, shipping, and more.

By eliminating the traditional players in the computer network and intermediaries, the common transaction risks are eliminated. For investors who believe in the power of new technology to shape the future, crypto investing is a very attractive option.

How to invest in cryptocurrency safely

If you choose to invest in cryptocurrency, the first thing to remember is to be strategic to avoid mistakes. Like any kind of investing, success is not guaranteed. And because cryptocurrency carries greater risks compared to investing in stocks, you need to have a certain ceiling on the amount of money you can afford to lose.

Make sure that you have an emergency fund or savings for your personal/family needs if something happened after you invested your extra fund in cryptocurrency. This is to avoid cashing your investment when the prevailing price in the market will not give you profits or worse, less than the amount you pay for the crypto coin.

✓ Research and learn about the popular and most beneficial cryptocurrencies before making a decision to purchase. Of course, Bitcoin and Ethereum are the best choices, but there are very promising altcoins that can give you short-term to long-term profits.

- ✓ Take time to get familiar with the industry or world of digital currencies-how it operates and works for investors and users.

- ✓ Explore and study how blockchain technology empowers cryptocurrencies.

- ✓ Join online forums and communities of crypto enthusiasts to become more updated about the market trends and the latest news about crypto.

- ✓ Read the white paper of the cryptocurrency, which is accessible on the website. If there is no available white paper or if it seems a bit odd because of misleading or absence of crucial information, move to the next crypto on your list.

If you're thinking of buying crypto in an ICO (initial coin offering), reading the company's prospectus is important. Remember that for any crypto project, the widespread adoption of investors is important. Failing to gain good numbers of supporters and users is a red flag and can lead to loss of investment. But while there are failed crypto projects, many have survived the 'birthing period' and are now thriving well in the market.

Check the following information:

- o *Who is the owner (or owners) of the company?* If the people behind the project are well-known and trusted names in the industry, it is a good sign.

- o *Who are the major investors of the company or project?*

- o *Is the company raising money to produce the crypto or already developed?* The status level of the project/product is important to consider.

- o *What will you have in exchange for your investment? Is it a coin, token, or a stake in the company?* (Stake ownership involves receiving a share of earning, a token is a utility currency that allows you to vote or redeem for a special purpose, and the crypto coin is a currency you can use for digital transactions

By doing these things, you will better understand how your investment will work for you. In the end, the best investment is the one that grows over time and promises great returns when it's time to sell it to another investor.

Are you ready to invest?

When you have covered all the fundamental steps that smart investors do prior to investing, your next move is to know when to buy your first crypto coin or coins. The digital world is fast-paced and volatile, hence the right timing is the key to your purchasing success.

The prices of crypto tend to follow a certain pattern. More often than not, other cryptocurrencies follow the general trajectory of Bitcoin. To date, Bitcoin remains the leading virtual currency in the industry. Monitoring the price movement is crucial to investing. Any news or rumors of price manipulation, exchange hack, fraud, and so on can crash the selling price of crypto. Purchasing hot new crypto before it sells like hotcakes due to popularity and growth of value is a nice move.

To protect yourself and your investment, here are additional tips for your perusal:

> Check everything before leaping. It basically means that before you invest your hard-earned money to buy this hot commodity called crypto, learn how it works, how to buy and sell it, and how to leverage its value.

> Choose the right digital wallet to protect your crypto. There are different types of electronic wallets to suit your

preferences. You can go for a hot wallet or cold wallet. Hot wallet requires Internet connectivity to access your crypto, while cold The software wallets are also categorized as mobile wallets, desktop wallets, or web wallets. Hardware wallets are the best option for HODLers (long-term investors) and those who want more secure storage for their investment.

➢ Prepare your backup strategy. In any kind of investing, you need a plan and plan B to mitigate loss.

Key Point

Financial experts describe cryptocurrency as a transformative technology with tremendous potential and power to revolutionize various industries. It is often compared to what the Internet has done way back 1990s. The breakthrough technology created a ripple of change as well as new industries and new types of jobs across the globe.

2020: The turnaround year for cryptocurrencies

No one has ever predicted that Bitcoin and other cryptocurrencies would have a blast in 2020. The virtual currencies, even the strongest ones like Bitcoin, were all trying to push through the prolonged price slump. During that time, institutional investors were not keen on adding crypto to their financial portfolio and the market liquidity was low.

And the pandemic happened. Investors, private and corporate, became extremely comprehensive about the multiple rounds of central banks' stimulus spending and began looking for ways to stabilize their investments. Crypto investing turned to be a great option and shook the price stupor. As the demand continued escalating, the price of Bitcoin and altcoins skyrocketed. There was a general price growth of 200%.

But as I said, the crypto market is volatile and unpredictable. In September 2020, Bitcoin price went up from $10,764 to $64,829, and then again spiraled down to more than $40,000. Fast forward this 2021, the year is another breakthrough year for cryptocurrency. Amidst the ongoing pandemic, they continue to grow strong in terms of prices, adoption, and popularity among investors.   Once again,

Bitcoin dominated the scene and was followed by Ethereum.

Being the largest crypto in the context of market cap, Bitcoin has become a strong indicator of market trends and movements. Speculations can crash its standing and price or boost its popularity, demand, and price.

Monitoring the market price of popular crypto as well as the fastest-growing new cryptocurrencies or tokens is a must-do for investors. The market of virtual currencies is highly volatile, displaying uptrends and downtrends that can impact your profit or loss.

The future of cryptocurrency

Potential or speculation – these two terms are common in the world of cryptocurrency. Investors and traders see the potential of crypto while speculations influence the uptrends and downtrends, the demand and supply, and the prices of the crypto coins or tokens. No one can accurately predict the future value of cryptocurrency. As a speculative investment, it does not offer have a solid history to base predictions. Even the self-proclaimed 'crypto guru' or experts can never tell how will Bitcoin or other cryptocurrencies behave in the coming days, weeks, months, or years.

Key takeaways

- Traditional and cryptocurrency investing are basically similar. The goal is to buy an asset/coin with strong potential to grow its value in time.

- Both have risks and rewards, albeit crypto investing is much more volatile and riskier.

- The future of Bitcoin and other cryptocurrencies remains speculative and in the hands of their holders.

- Before investing, it is crucial to understand the risk factors and the unique volatility of cryptocurrencies.

- Know your reasons why you are investing in Bitcoin or any other crypto and make them your guiding wisdom.

Point to Ponder

Keep learning and growing your worth. Investing in bitcoin-linked assets in the Stock market is one way to do it.

Chapter 4

Bitcoin and Stock Market

"A bitcoin ETF ratifies crypto relevancy in today's economy."
– Chris Kline (COO and co-founder of Bitcoin IRA)-

Is there a correlation between Bitcoin and the stock market?

Correlation refers to the statistical relationship (causal or not or the degree to which two random variables are linearly associated. For years, experts have been trying to discern the correlation of Bitcoin with the stock market. Many times in the past, when the prices of stocks skyrocketed, Bitcoin followed or vice versa.

However, during these pandemic months when the global stock markets are experiencing some setbacks, Bitcoin has recovered immensely and displayed new all-time highs. The recovery occurred without the backup of uptrends in the stock markets. This is an indication of a trend break, which is a characteristic of their correlated way. Sometimes they follow the same route, other times they move differently.

> Bitcoin is technically an uncorrelated "safe haven" asset.

> While Bitcoin has shown a correlation with the stock markets, gold, and other asset classes, it is independent and has its own pattern of uptrends and downtrends.

> Bitcoin gradually decoupled from the stock market since December 2020 and demonstrated an inverse correlation.

Take a look:

- The Vanguard Total World Stock ETF Price Development Chart for a 5-year period (October 6, 2021) showed that world stock markets and Bitcoin moved in the same direction from 2017 to the first part of 2021. Then, the pattern broke. Bitcoin suffered a slump during the beginning of 2021. The international stock market continued its good performance. In October 2021, Bitcoin showed a positive recovery. The stock market was still down.

- In the 10-year comparative chart issued on October 7, 2021, by Vanguard Total World Stock ETF, there were two instances when the stock market and Bitcoin were non-correlated. One was during the end of 2014 up to 2016 and the second was at the start of 2018. Bitcoin had serious corrections during both times while the stock market displayed slight movement.

Correlation is a two-way relationship for Bitcoin and stocks

The relation between Bitcoin and the stock market is two-way. While there are events and factors that impact the Bitcoin market movement, the growing interest of large institutions and their own market forces can also play a significant role in the global stock markets.

Factors that tie Bitcoin to stock prices

- **Emergence of digital-savvy investors -** They are bridging the gap that separates stock from cryptocurrency.

- **Similar participants** - It reaches the point where the crypto market and stock market have the same players or participants, making the correlations inevitable.

- **Institutional adoption** – The correlation continues as more major companies and institutions include Bitcoin on the balance sheets.

- **Bitcoin futures contracts** – The successful launching of Maryland Based ProShares Bitcoin Strategy ETF BITO has opened a safer venue for investors to indirectly invest in the popular cryptocurrency.

Quote

"It was a blockbuster, smash, home run debut."
– Eric Balchunas (Senior ETF Analyst, Bloomberg) on BITO-

On Spotlight: ProShares BITO

It is official, ProShares Bitcoin Strategy ETF with ticker symbol BITO is a certified blockbuster after hitting a massive $570 million in assets in one day and over $1 billion in assets under management (AUM) in two days when it made its debut on the New York Stock Exchange. It broke the 18-years, 3-day record of SPDR Gold Shares (GLD) as the fastest exchange-traded fund to reach a billion-dollar threshold.

Finally, it was a home run performance for Bitcoin futures after the grueling months of waiting for the Securities and Exchange Commission (SEC) to approve their application. ProShares, a Maryland-based provider of specialized exchange-traded products has successfully launched their bitcoin ETF BITO.

It hit a major milestone of getting into the mainstream on October 19, 2021. This pure Bitcoin future ETF has opened the floodgates for other cryptocurrencies to follow. Once again, Bitcoin has proved its winning ability to attract investors by offering a safer option for those who are wary of direct investing.

Should you join the BITO $1 billion pool?

As the first U.S. bitcoin-related exchange-traded fund (ETF), ProShares Bitcoin Strategy ETF (BITO) offers investors a chance to gain capital appreciation from future contracts. It provides a pure form of cryptocurrency exposure using a brokerage account, which means you gain exposure to the asset without needing to hold or trade it.

This allows conservative investors who prefer IRAs, brokerage accounts, and other traditional vehicles to have exposure to bitcoin in a transparent, convenient, and liquid way. Take note that BITO is not a direct investment in Bitcoin. The performance and the price of bitcoin futures are different from the 'spot' price of bitcoins. The spot price is the current price of physical bitcoins in the exchange platforms or brokers.

Futures contracts are Bitcoin's derivative and are not directly linked or backed up by physical bitcoins. Also, their prices do not necessarily correlate with the bitcoin's price.

- *If the price of Bitcoin increases by 30%, the bitcoin futures ETFs may rise only 20%. The explanation of this is – "bitcoin futures are contracts with expiration and need to be repurchased," which gives a margin of tracking error between the underlying asset (bitcoin) and the ETF.*

In context, BITO is almost similar to the U.S. Oil Fund (USO) as it also invests in futures contracts without necessarily tracking the prevailing oil price. Instead, it tracks down SPDR Gold Shares (GLD) that directly invest in an underlying asset or product for more accurate price tracking. Futures-based products can also replicate the underlying market's performance and as the asset managers roll the contracts forward, they incur costs hence the expense ratio charge during their maturity period.

The futures contracts that this ETF invests in are traded and subject to the internal rules of the Chicago Mercantile Exchange. Being a short-term investment vehicle for cash position, the exchange-traded fund (ETF) BITO can also invest in U.S. Treasury Bills and Repurchase Agreements.

Bitcoin futures are also subject to unique risks which include lack of liquidity and price volatility. Like any other asset class, its principal value and returns may fluctuate so the value can be less or more than the original value.

Before you buy shares, always remember the key rule in investing- "only invest the money you that you can kiss goodbye if unexpected happens." In the end, bitcoin futures contracts are the middle ground that bridges the gap between traditional investing and cryptocurrency.

Other differences between buying Bitcoin from BITO

Fees

- When you buy physical bitcoin, you will be charged with certain fees.
- When you purchase specialized ETFs like BITO, expect an expense ratio of 0.95% for every $10,000 investment.

Regulations

- Bitcoin operates on its own rules.
- Bitcoin-linked ETF BITO comes with better protection. Brokerage accounts are covered by the Securities Investor Protection Corporation (SIPC), providing up to $500,000 insurance when the firm shuts down because of financial difficulties that lead to missing assets of customers and bankruptcy.

Market hours

- Bitcoin is not subject to any kind of market hours. You can purchase, sell, or trade your bitcoins whenever you want.
- BITO can be purchased within the market hours of brokerages or exchanges. If you place your order during an off-market hour, it will be fulfilled when the stock market opens. Also, BITO transactions are not available during evenings or weekends.

The journey of bitcoin futures to the stock market

It took about 8 years of failures to finally have a crypto-tied ETF in the stock markets. But the idea that Bitcoin and ETFs would eventually meet has been there all along since these two areas of investment provide a conducive growing environment in terms of profits. Exchange-traded funds (ETFs) are a popular form of investment in the stock market and Bitcoin is known for generating huge profits.

But the journey is not easy and has some growing pains. The SEC's hesitancy to embrace crypto assets is based on the concerns of potential manipulation and fraud as well as lack of regulations over the Bitcoin market. Many companies have tried to seek approval for their bitcoin ETF applications from this regulatory body, but generally, the U.S. regulators are extremely careful in reviewing them. Most of the unapproved applications are based on spot markets or direct investing in cryptocurrency. The first attempt was filed in 2013 by the famous twins Cameron and Tyler Winklevoss. Their petition to launch Winklevoss Bitcoin Trust was disapproved by the SEC in 2017.

The shift happened sometime in August of 2021 when SEC Chairman Gary Gensler announced that the agency would be considering the futures-backed bitcoin ETFs under the provisions of the Investment Company Act of 1940. It resulted in a flood of applications.

What you should know before investing in bitcoin futures ETFs?

After the successful launching of BITO, the interest of investors escalated. It was like Christmas in October when large-volume and high-frequency traders/investors wanted to be part of the bigger picture.

While this ETF correlates with bitcoin, it does not mirror the value of the cryptocurrency. It will be tracking the future contracts' price which can be incredibly unpredictable like the physical coins. It is important to be mentally and emotionally prepared for volatility issues.

Bitcoin futures and bitcoin cryptocurrency are different from each other. When you invest in bitcoin futures, you are buying or selling bitcoin. You are buying or selling the asset from a broker or exchange provider in the future at a specified date and price. It can be immensely dangerous if the bitcoin futures ETFs occupy a huge portion of your financial portfolio. Start small and see how it will perform, then gradually increase if you enjoy the challenge of massive price swings.

When the set date arrives, investors must buy or sell the underlying asset at the specified price. If the amount of bitcoin during that day is high, you get a good profit. This is known as *"trading at a premium."* However, if the bitcoin's price is low than what you are expecting, you lose some money. It is *"trading at a discount."*

Bitcoin ETFs and Bitcoin Futures explained

Bitcoin ETF mimics the movement of the world's popular digital currency price. This investment vehicle tracks the performance of bitcoins. It also allows investment diversification without the need for investors to own the asset, do the complex trading process by themselves, or practice safe storage of bitcoins. It is a perfect alternative for people who only focus on the gains or losses of investing.

> ➢ Generally, ETFs offer a simpler option to buy and sell individual assets or stocks representing a larger basket of commodities that help investors diversify their holdings.

Bitcoin futures provides investors to gain exposure to the digital gold of virtual currency without holding it under their safekeeping. It works like the traditional futures contracts for a stock index or a commodity, allowing investors to speculate on the future price without holding the underlying asset.

Investors of bitcoin futures can take cash settlement rather than physical bitcoin delivery during the contract settlement. The first entity that offered this type of contract was the Cboe Options Exchange on December 10, 2017. However, it stopped offering new bitcoin futures contracts in March 2019.

Here are the active exchanges that offer cash settlement or physical bitcoin delivery:

- **CME or Chicago Mercantile Exchange** offers cash for monthly futures contracts. It started the bitcoin futures platform on December 18, 2017. It also offers *options on bitcoin futures* and *Micro Bitcoin futures* (one-tenth the size of bitcoin).

- **Intercontinental Exchange and Bakkt** offer monthly or daily bitcoin futures contracts for *physical delivery*. In the context of futures or options contracts, physical delivery refers to the transfer of the underlying asset of the contract on a predetermined date from the hands of the seller/provider to the buyer.

How does Bitcoin Futures work?

When you invest in Bitcoin Futures, you are buying cash-settled, **front-month** futures contracts or agreements to sell/buy the asset in the future at a predetermined price at a predetermined date, instead of investing in bitcoin directly. The term "front-month" means that the contracts will be maturing soon and once they do, the ETF will be buying up contracts for the next month.

Let's take CME Group bitcoin futures as an example:

- Contract unit is 5 bitcoin (BTC) and paid in US dollars
- Listed contracts for 6 consecutive months and 2 additional Decembers
- Margin requirement is 50% cash of the contract amount
- Settlement method is financially-settled

Let's say the price of bitcoin when you purchase your bitcoin futures contract is $10,000. Since each contract unit has 5 bitcoins, your total investment would be $50,000. The required margin at CME is 50%, so you have to deposit $25,000 and finance the remaining balance of the futures contract by using leverage.

Take note that the value of the futures contract follows the price of its underlying asset, which in this case is bitcoin. CME uses the Bitcoin Reference Rate to calculate the bitcoin's volume-weighted average price every day between 3:00-4:00 p.m. London time. The average price is calculated from different exchanges.

During uncertainties like price fluctuations, you have the option to sell your future contract to another investor or hold onto it. When the contract matures, you let it expire and collect your cash or roll it over by buying a new contract.

How can investors leverage their bitcoin futures?

For the variety of players in the ecosystem of Bitcoin, futures contracts deliver different purposes. Each purpose is unique to the particular group of participants.

- Investors can short their bitcoin futures as a hedge. This means that even if the price of the bitcoins moves adversely, they still make profits in the spot market.

- Active traders and speculators in the stock market who enjoy moving in and out of future trades can use the contracts for long and short-term profits.

- Bitcoin miners can use futures to lock in the prices and guarantee a hefty return on their investments.

Pros and Cons of bitcoin futures

Pros

- ✓ **Better liquidity in futures markets** – The futures markets have more liquidity and deeper volume compared to the crypto markets.

- ✓ **Door for institutional investors** – It is another venue where institutional investors can buy Bitcoin to add to their financial portfolios. Bitcoin futures are traded on the Commodity Futures Trading Commission-regulated exchanges.

✓ **Lower fees** – Bitcoin investing can be expensive due to the cost and transaction fees. Bitcoin ETF is a low-fee option than buying physical bitcoins or investing in Grayscale Bitcoin Trust (GBTC) which is known for an annual 2.0% charge

✓ **Safer option** – Bitcoin ETF eliminates the issues of complex security and storage procedures that are typically required from investors of physical bitcoins. Bitcoin wallet is not necessary because futures contracts are cash-settled.

✓ **Short-sell ability** – Investors can easily short sell their ETF shares if they see that the value of bitcoins will decline in the future.

✓ **Less risk exposure** - Future contracts have price limits and position limits, enabling investors to avoid risks.

Cons

- ○ **Cost of carry** – The price of futures is dependent on the current spot price and the pre-delivery cost of carry which can be positive or negative. The cost of carry is subject to the supply and demand that stem from the anticipated pricing of future events.

- ○ **Contango** – The state of Bitcoin contango refers to the situation where the forward price of the futures price is higher than its spot price. It usually manifests when there is a strong expectation that the price of the commodity will rise over time.

Other Bitcoin ETFs and Futures-based crypto funds

A. Bitcoin ETFs

There were 13 Bitcoin ETFs applications waiting for the stamp of approval from the SEC in July 2021. ProShares ETF BITO was the first one to get the much-awaited "Yes" of the body. Three days after the successful launch of BITO, Valkyrie Bitcoin Strategy ETF went public, too. On November,

- **Valkyrie ETF** (BTF, $24.30)

  This Tennessee-based alternative asset manager specializes in both traditional and digital assets. It has been selling trusts for crypto including Bitcoin, but its BTF is the first crypto ETF. Valkyrie is also eyeing to launch more bitcoin futures ETFs in the coming days.

  In a way, BTF is like BITO since it invests in CME Bitcoin futures through the Cayman Islands subsidiary and it charges an expense ratio of 0.95%. However, actively-managed BTF failed to receive the same warm response that BITO had during the launching as it only accumulated $5 million in assets under management (AUM).

- **VanEck Bitcoin Futures ETF** (XBTF)

  This is the third bitcoin futures ETF that went public. It started trading under the XBTF ticker on November 15, 2021, on the CBOE Exchange. It has a 0.65% net expense ratio and is actively managed.

  It is currently the cheapest bitcoin-linked exchange-traded fund with a structure like a C-Corporation. According to the firm's top executives, it may offer a more efficient tax incentive for investors who are opting for long-term holdings.

B. Futures-based crypto funds

- **Amplify Transformational Data Sharing ETF** (BLOK, $48.62)

  It is currently the largest ETF in the market today with actively-managed $1.3 billion worth of assets with a 0.71% expense ratio. It primarily invests in equities and offers more "direct" exposure in companies that develop blockchain technology or use it for their business operation.

  It has 47 holdings with the top 10 comprising 45% of assets. As of November 15, 2021, the list includes:

  - Silvergate Capital Corp Ordinary Shares - Class A SI
  - Galaxy Digital Holdings Ltd. GLXY
  - Coinbase Global Inc. Ordinary Shares Class A COIN
  - Hut 8 Mining Corp. New Com CA HUT
  - Nvidia Corp NVDA
  - Riot Blockchain Inc
  - Marathon Digital Holdings Inc. MARA
  - Hive Blockchain Technologies CA HIVE

- Bitfarms Ltd/Canada CA: BITF
- CME Group Inc.

Other BLOK holdings outside the list but directly track the performance of Bitcoin include the 31Q CoinShares Bitcoin ETF and the Purpose Bitcoin ETF. BLOK's expense ratio is 0.71%.

- **Siren Nasdaq NexGen Economy ETF** (BLCN $46.12)

This passively-managed index exchange-traded fund (ETF) boasts $291 million in assets. BLCN holds more stocks than BLOK. It has 63 holdings of companies with over $200 million in market capitalization and exhibits characteristics of a "blockchain company." It has a 0.68% expense ratio.

BLCN utilizes a "blockchain score", the proprietary screening method of index that scores the company's ability to get the most out from the blockchain technology.

As of November 15, 2021, the largest holdings that account for 20% of the overall assets, came from the following companies.

- o Bakkt Holdings Inc. Ordinary Shares - Class A BAKKT
- o Silvergate Capital Corp Ordinary Shares - Class A SI
- o Marathon Digital Holdings Inc. MARA
- o Galaxy Digital Holdings Ltd. GLXY
- o Overstock.com Inc. OSTK
- o Microstrategy Inc. Ordinary Share A MSTR
- o NCIVIA Corp NVDA
- o Coinbase Global Inc. Ordinary Shares Class A COIN
- o Advanced Micro Devices Inc. AMD
- o Accenture PLC Ordinary Shares Class A CAN

- **Bitwise 10 Crypto Index Fund** (BITW $50.25)

With $1.2 billion assets under management, BITW tracks the performance of 10 investable crypto in the Bitwise 10 Large Cap Crypto Index which accounts for 70% of the entire market of cryptocurrency. It is weighted by market cap so it is not surprising that 65% of its portfolio are Bitcoin accounts, followed by Ethereum (25%), and Cardano (4%).

The over-the-counter availability of BITW that started in December 2020 made it highly popular and in less than one year, the $120 million in assets increased ten times. NITW's expense ratio is 2.50%.

- **Simplify US Equity PLUS GBTC ETF** (SPBC $26.89)

  SPBC has 111.0 million in assets with a 0.50% expense ratio. It offers 100% investment in equities and 10% Bitcoin exposure. By providing both in the stock market and crypto, Simplify US Equity has become a popular asset management company. It mostly invests in iShares Core S& P 500 ETF (IVV), partly in E-mini S&P 500 Futures, and Grayscale Bitcoin Trust.

- **First Trust Indxx Innovative Transaction & Process ETF (**LEGR, $43.03)

  This equity-based crypto ETF tracks the Indxx Blockchain Index, which in turn follows the performance of blockchain-linked companies. It also uses a weighting method to gauge the blockchain companies in terms of size, trading minimums, and liquidity.

- A score of 1 is for firms that are actively developing blockchain
- A score of 2 is for companies that are actively using blockchain
- A score of 3 is for those that are actively exploring blockchain

This ETF has $135.3 million in assets with an expense ratio of 0.65%. It has an approximately $94 billion median market cap, being a large-cap heavy fund.

- **Bitwise Crypto Industry Innovators ETF (**BITQ, $23.95)

    As equity-focused crypto exchange-traded funds, it tracks the Bitwise Crypto Innovators 30 Index. It has $80.8 million in assets with a 0.85% expense ratio. For companies to be listed in the index, they should have 75% net holdings in bitcoin (other kinds of liquid cryptocurrency) or 75% of revenue is generated from the crypto ecosystem.

Hot crypto stocks to invest in for the next Bitcoin rush

When Bitcoin's price dropped to $30,000 in late May from $64,000 new-high in mid-April, it dragged down a lot of crypto stocks and altcoins. Then it had a quick rebound to around

$40,000 and the current price is playing between around the range of $30,000 and $40,000. This development sustained the high interest of traders and investors in virtual currencies, bitcoin-linked ETFs, and blockchain technology-backed companies in the stock market.

The digital reforms are partly due to the pandemic, with many companies leveraging the secure authentication technology or blockchain and accepting Bitcoin as payment for the services or goods.

Stock markets have also leveraged the potentials of these digital currencies by offering bitcoin futures to investors who are looking forward to diversifying their portfolio as well as earning short-term to long-term profits.

Here are the top cryptocurrency stocks that investors should have to prepare for the Bitcoin boom:

1. PayPal Holdings (PYPL $288.12)

According to the survey of Mizuho Securities to 380 PayPal users, 17% answered that they are using the platform to purchase or sell their crypto. Putting it in a large perspective, this 17%

translates to 67 million people out of its 392 million users across the world.

In a letter sent to their shareholders, hedge fund and investment company Pantera Capital shared that PayPal is buying over 100% of newly-issued bitcoins and Square's Cash App. This is a clear indication that crypto functionality is now recognized in the finance world and Bitcoin as a digital store of value.

Wall Street experts collectively believe that PayPal will be averaging an annual growth of 24.1% growth in the next 3-5 years. PayPal's market value is now $333.5 billion with a 1,206% earnings growth rate quarterly. Its profit margin is 22.8% while the return on equity - trailing 12 months (TTM) is 29.4%.

2. Square (SQ $238.70)

This card-reading hardware payment company has purchased 4,709 bitcoins amounting to $50 million. It is also a leading company in the stock markets that allow investors to buy, deposit, withdraw, and store bitcoins through its Cash App. It also added Auto Invest, a feature that allows dollar-cost averaging on a set schedule of weekly or daily purchases of stocks or bitcoins.

Square's current market value is $108.7 billion. It has allocated $170 million to bitcoins during the 1st quarter of 2021. During the 3rd quarter of the year, Cash App earned $3.5 billion in bitcoin-related transactions. Square's profit margin is 2.7% while the return on equity is 17.4%.

3. MicroStrategy(MSTR $533.00)

With a market value of $5.4 billion, MicroStrategy is the brainchild of Michael Saylor. He was only 24 when he started this company, making him one of the pioneering tech founders in the industry.

Once a small player, this data analytics company managed to get to the trillion-dollars list after making a strategic move to replace the cash with Bitcoin on the balance sheet. It spent approximately $3 billion to buy crypto, which resulted in a 370% growth in assets.

While enjoying the Bitcoin boom during the past months, MSTR moved further by transferring the volatility of the digital currencies to shares of stocks. It is moving forward with full steam, offering crypto stocks that you should be watching closely to leverage your investment potentials.

4. JPMorgan Chase(JPM $151.12)

JPM's CEO Jamie Dimon is not keen on Bitcoin. During the 2017 boom, he called Bitcoin a "fraud" and last year he said it is still "not his cup of tea." He is known as one of the most outspoken skeptics of digital assets on Wall Street.

However, he is supportive of blockchain technology and even letting the clients of the house of Morgan invest in Bitcoin Fun that NYDIG has created. In late July, JPMorgan has quietly rolled out access to 5 funds – the Grayscale Bitcoin Trust, Grayscale Bitcoin Cash Trust, Grayscale Ethereum Classic Trust, Grayscale Ethereum Trust, and Osprey Bitcoin Trust.

Recently, Dimon said that *"their clients are interested and he doesn't tell clients what to do."* If this is a sign of an eroding resistance in Bitcoin and other cryptocurrencies, Wall Street is waiting for him to concede.

5. Advanced Micro Devices (AMD $83.82)

AMD played well during the recent digital gold rush and has gone up near $100 per share during mid-January before settling in the range of mid-$80s. Nonetheless, it remains strong enough with its 242.6% quarterly earnings growth rate.

The company benefits from the high demand of crypto miners for high-performance computer processors. It reported a 93% year-over-year revenue increase during the 1st quarter of 2021. Stock analysts are optimistic about AMD with its market value of $101.8%, profit margin of 25.2%, and 60.6% return on equity.

6. Nvidia (NVDA $762.29)

Bitcoin mining has created a constant demand for the most high-powered computer processors, making NVIDIA's market value rise up to $474.9 billion with a quarterly earnings growth rate of 108.5%. Its profit margin is 27.7% while the return on equity is 33.4%

Nvidia also released its new generation of processors exclusively for crypto mining.

During the first quarter of 2021, its crypto mining cards have generated a revenue of $155 million. And while it is not the purest crypto stock, NVDA always enjoys the boost from Bitcoin's boom.

7. Coinbase Global (COIN $226.01)

This brokerage company has been selling and trading bitcoins and other major altcoins then collecting fees for the transactions. It always makes bigger revenue and profits whenever the price of Bitcoin drops, making the "buy the dip" crypto buyers excited to get hold of this crypto coin.

It also launched Coinbase Prime, which has opened more opportunities to institutional investors. The unit ties data analytics, custody services, and trading together. COIN stocks are likely to become bigger and stronger.

Coinbase Global has a market value of $59.2 billion, 2,313% quarterly earnings growth rate, profit margin of 36.8%, and a 54.2% return on equity.

8. Grayscale Bitcoin Trust (GBTC $27.79)

With $21.9 billion assets under management, this investment company allows you to buy GBTC shares and tracks down the Bitcoin's price you hold but like ETFs, you cannot cash in the shares of stocks for physical bitcoins. GBTC is also not traded on any major exchange platforms, but "over the counter."

Key takeaways

- Bitcoin had early patterns of correlation with the stock market. An inverse correlation eventually decoupled them.

- The successful launching of ProShares BITO was a major milestone for Bitcoin-linked futures.

- Aside from Bitcoin futures, investing in hot crypto stocks is a ticket to leverage the opportunities in the next bull market.

Chapter 5

Guide to Bitcoin Investing: Let's Gear You Up

"It's money 2.0." – *Chamath Palihapitiva*

The impressive 763% growth of Bitcoin valuation within a span of one year made it the much-sought 'digital gold' among today's investors. The debates over its future in the investing sphere have ceased at this juncture, thanks to the large institutional investors and high-profile people who jumped into the bandwagon.

Undoubtedly, Bitcoin momentum is building up and attracting more individuals and companies. The recent developments and meteoric rise of its value have convinced many people that it is the just beginning of a golden journey for Bitcoin holders.

Investing in Bitcoin has become a fast wealth-building vehicle. But remember that just like traditional investments, it has its pitfalls and traps that can lead to losing instead of winning. It is easy to get excited as you explore the new realm and its opportunities, so here are some tips to live by:

1. **Start small** - The first and most important rule is to 'buy bitcoins within your limits' or the amount you can afford to let go without affecting your savings or living expenses. Create a budget for Bitcoin investing. The safest ceiling is not more than 10% of your financial portfolio. Perhaps, investing $10 every week is a healthy start. It is also fun seeing your Bitcoin investment grow week after week.

2. **Know your risk tolerance** – Bitcoin remains a high-risk investment asset, so it is necessary to check your risk tolerance before you start investing in cryptocurrency. If you are not comfortable buying volatile assets or you cannot afford to invest a lot of money, then go for the other investment options.

3. **Diversify your financial portfolio** – Wise men say, 'never put all your golden eggs in one basket.' It is true in investment, so always protect yourself and your family from investment loss by portfolio diversification. You should have low-risk primary investments (index funds, government bonds), medium-risk investments (corporate stocks, real-estate stocks), and high-risk investments (Bitcoin, altcoins). Bitcoin investment is your portfolio's 'icing on the cake' that has a potential promise of giving you a 'sweet luxury and fortune' and if it doesn't, your future is still fine.

Bitcoin as an investment asset

Bitcoin is an investment asset class of its own, proving its capacity to grow in value after going 20-fold times since 2018. But its magnitude does not end there, since this 'king of crypto' can transcend the borders of investing. It helps investors diversify their portfolios and is paired concurrently with other assets.

A. Bitcoin and Real Estate

There is a new concept in real estate called 'tokenization.' It refers to the process of producing a virtual token to represent the ownership of interest. The token exists on the Bitcoin blockchain, offering real estate investors to have more investment options and earn substantial profits. This unique convergence of Bitcoin and real estate companies has great potential to revolutionize the existing domestic and global markets.

Real estate tokenization gives an opportunity to people to explore the crypto world by allowing fractional ownership of residential or commercial property. To buy a real estate token, investors must participate in an initial coin offering. It operates by dividing the property value into multiple virtual tokens where individual and institutional investors are waiting to purchase a piece of the pie. The tokenization process utilized smart contracts.

156

Benefits of tokenization

> **Increased liquidity** – Real estate investment is an illiquid asset or has low-liquidity characteristics because of significant capital requirement, tedious paperwork, and involvement of various parties. With tokenization, the property gets fractionalized and allows small investors or beginners to be part of the leading industry that generates real nice revenue.

> **Immutable proof of right or ownership** – Tokenization eliminates the battle over rights and ownership of the property. With data in the blockchain ledger, no one can tamper the documents. It is also easy to access once the fractional or sole ownership has been declared.

> **Market access** – When it comes to real estate investment, there is no denying that it is a game for the rich and famous who want to own remarkable properties. However, with tokenization, everyone interested can have a fraction of the asset and hold or sell it to interested buyers from any part of the world.

> **Less expensive** – Since the transaction requires less administrative work and intermediaries, the whole process costs

less than conventional real estate transactions.

➢ **Transparent** – All details of the transaction, contract clauses, due dates, and other necessary information are programmed into a digital token, making them transparent to sellers and investors.

➢ **Easy management of the property** – Tokens and smart contracts in the blockchain streamline the process of lease renewal or monthly payment collection. With real estate tokenization, registered investors in the database get timely payments from tenants.

Wise thoughts

Real estate tokenization has an incredibly bright future. It is only a matter of time before all assets are blockchain- based assets.

-Graeme Moore-
Polymath head of tokenization-

B. Bitcoin IRAs

Bitcoin IRAs are special retirement accounts that offer higher returns as well as diversify the retirement portfolio. But then, before jumping on board and adding this type of retirement plan, remember that anything related to Bitcoin has risks and volatility issues. It is also crucial to understand what a Bitcoin IRA is.

In a nutshell, a Bitcoin IRA is a self-directed individual retirement account that allows people to invest in a variety of alternative asset classes (precious metals, real estate, and cryptocurrency.) It works like other IRAs, but with a little DIY. The Bitcoin IRA providers can partner with a crypto exchange or let you trade your Bitcoin in a 3rd-party crypto exchange.

Some of the popular providers of Bitcoin IRAs are BitIRA, Alto, Bitcoin IRA, Equity Trust, IRA Financial Trust, BlockMint, and iTrustCapital.

C. Standalone Bitcoin

The collective craze around Bitcoin is hard to ignore. And while it is also difficult to predict if it will be bigger than it is now and become a store of value or a global reserve currency in the future, it is now widely accepted as the 'digital gold' of modern times. Many are chasing the opportunity of massive profits that it offers while the others are still in quandary between the thrill of becoming rich or ruin.

When someone asks me if Bitcoin is a good investment, my answer is always in the affirmative. Because I do believe that like any other form of investment, the key to successful management is diligence. The way you handle your investment asset defines success and failure.

Traditional investors and institutions have already realized Bitcoin's ability to disrupt the conventional methods in the financial world. Many chose to adopt and integrate crypto into their vault of riches instead of facing irrelevance. As we are seeing it, the elite group and people with a healthy appetite for risks are leading the pack of Bitcoin supporters. They believed in its future and those who risked years ago have already reaped their millions or billions. As long as the global markets favor and chase Bitcoin, it will continue its phenomenal performance and attract more investors. Soon enough, when the last bitcoin is mined, it will be harder to buy and the demand will grow despite the presence of other cryptocurrencies.

To buy or not to buy Bitcoin

Investing in Bitcoin is a personal choice. The stronger is your appetite for challenges and risks, the higher is your interest to buy bitcoins.

Top reasons why you should buy Bitcoin

The main attraction is Bitcoin investing is you can generate a monumental return on profits, more than 100% of your capital investment. The more bitcoins you have in your portfolio, the higher is your opportunity to capitalize on market surges and sell them to crypto investors. You can generate huge profits as high as 300% if you have a large volume of Bitcoin by capitalizing on the market uptrends.

Bitcoin is also incredibly liquid because of the presence of online crypto exchanges, brokerages, and trading platforms worldwide. It is now easier to trade bitcoins for another asset like gold or cash, with low transaction fees. Bitcoin is an outstanding investment vessel whether you are looking for long-term investment or short-term profits.

It is being adopted by big businesses and institutions, becoming more mainstream. With modern software, carrying out Bitcoin transactions becomes automatic and fast which is favorable for entrepreneurs and merchants.

This crypto is immune to inflation. It is not affected by the changes in the monetary and fiscal policy that causes the dollar valuation to decline and result in a high inflation rate.

Bitcoin's blockchain technology is infinite and your investment is secured as long as you do not lose your private keys to access it. It is reported that about 3.7 million BTCs were lost because the owners can no longer access them.

You can also try Bitcoin trading, which is simple and instant. Simply buy your desired volume of bitcoins and hold them in your digital wallet. When you want to sell them, place an offer to let the users of the exchange know that you are disposing of your coins. But for this, you must be careful when to enter and exit the market.

Finally, it brings new opportunities for ordinary people to invest. For so long, investing is an activity that is limited to financial specialists and individuals with big capital to spend. Bitcoin is relatively young and this newness is a strong factor that causes volatility and unpredictable price swings that can bring massive profits.

Top arguments why you should not buy Bitcoin

Bitcoin price is always going back and forth. While there was an astounding 7,875% return for those who sold their coins until May 2021, the guarantee that it would perform similar valuation growth for another 5 years is unlikely. But then, it all depends on several factors including wider adoption of investors. You could lose your assets if you do not practice due diligence and precautions.

Cryptocurrencies, including Bitcoin, are susceptible to the "pump-and-dump" schemes. Beware of predatory investors who are on the lookout for amateurs on Bitcoin investing. Their modus is to convince the newbies to invest more money to cause surges that would rapidly increase the Bitcoin price. And while the unsuspecting investors are busy buying bitcoins, the predatory investors would sell their coins during the surge and earn huge profits. When the preys stop buying, the price of Bitcoin will be extremely low so they have no choice but to hold them until the next surge. Pyramid schemes are also rampant in the crypto industry, so be conscious of 'so-called investors' who will try to attract your attention to be part of their crypto team by offering huge returns.

The risk of hacking is always present. One way to have peace of mind is holding custody of your account's private key. And don't ever lose it or you will be saying goodbye to your bitcoins forever.

Many governments are trying to crack down on Bitcoin-related businesses. China totally banned cryptocurrencies, while others have a friendlier stance but are still finding ways to regulate them. The crackdown and other regulatory policies that authorities are placing to protect investors in their jurisdictions cause the value of Bitcoin to decrease.

4 Steps to follow when buying bitcoins

Step 1: Decide whether you will buy from a Bitcoin exchange or a Bitcoin stockbroker.

Step 2: Decide where to store your Bitcoin.

Step 3: Buy your bitcoins.

Step 4: Manage your Bitcoin investment based on your long-term plans.

Pro tips:

- ✓ HODlers who want to make mid-term or long-term investments mostly use crypto exchanges to buy Bitcoin.

- ✓ Speculative investors who want to explore various types of trading, TA instruments, and investment tools use crypto exchanges. They see brokers as a medium for their mid-term or short-term goals.

- ✓ When choosing a cryptocurrency exchange for long-term investment, consider the advanced options (DeFi tokens, crypto indices), bonuses and commissions, and cool perks they offer.

164

Bitcoin brokers versus Bitcoin exchanges

Bitcoins are available through crypto exchanges and brokers. They make profits from the service fees paid by their clients.

- **Bitcoin brokers** offer cryptocurrencies and other derivatives like options, futures, and CFDs. They act as mediators between the market and the traders or investors. Crypto brokers usually offer lower trading and withdrawal fees.

  Brokers allow investors to trade their virtual assets without owning them. The brokers allow the crypto sellers to set the price and fee. They can hold the funds for you and collaborate with other brokers to ensure a sufficient supply of bitcoins and other cryptocurrencies. To leverage the demand, they are more likely to sell virtual coins and tokens at prices that are similar to other brokers.

  Examples of digital currency brokers:

  - ✓ **Robinhood Markets, Inc. (HOOD)** – It is the first investment broker that sells bitcoins. This broker firm does not charge commission fees for purchases and trades of cryptocurrencies. It makes profits from passing the trading volume to other brokerages or trading platforms (payment for order flow).

- ✓ **eToro** – Its social trading platform allows crypto users to match the trading moves of experienced traders.

- ✓ **TradeStation** – It offers bitcoin and altcoin trading.

- **Bitcoin exchanges** are platforms that sell Bitcoin and other cryptocurrencies. They act as intermediaries, enabling the trade and charging fees for their services. Fees for deposits, withdrawals, and trades are usually high. Most of them have their own exchange wallets, giving you an option to leave your digital assets for their safekeeping. You may also store your crypto outside the platform for better peace of mind.

In these platforms, there are multiple sellers and buyers who are simultaneously placing their offers to purchase or dispose of their cryptocurrencies. They match sellers with buyers, allowing any buyer to select the price that fits his budget and offers an intention to buy. Once the seller agrees, the order will be fulfilled and the transaction is completed.

Users can input a limit order or a market order when buying or selling bitcoins. If the buyer or seller chooses the limit order, the exchange will trade coins above the current bid price or below the current asking price. On the other hand, a market order authorizes the exchange platform to trade bitcoins in the marketplace for the most profitable price.

To deposit funds, users can use different options such as direct bank transfers, bank wires, bank drafts, money orders, debit or credit cards, and gift cards. For withdrawal purposes, check the options they provide which may include bank wire, credit card transfers, PayPal transfer, cash delivery, bank transfer, or check mailing.

There are two types of exchange:

1. *Centralized exchange* – They are online platforms that let you create an account by providing login details. You can transfer funds (fiat or crypto) from your bank account to fund your crypto wallet and make a transaction. In this type of exchange, the

governing organization creates and sets rules regarding the information to be shared in the platform, what can be traded, and the withdrawal limits.

Examples of centralized exchanges are *Binance, Coinbase, Gemini, and CoinMama.*

✓ **Coinbase** – U.S. buyers mostly prefer using Coinbase because it can easily be linked in the bank accounts. It also has a wide choice of altcoins. Every transaction is charged with a 0.5% spread (or the adjustment in the sale or purchase price of your investment) and a service fee which is variable depending on the mode of payment and location.

✓ **Binance** – It has the biggest collection of available cryptocurrencies and charges a 0.1% fee plus withdrawal fee. It also offers a wide range of cryptocurrency-to-cryptocurrency trading pairs. Binance is best for advanced traders and investors.

✓ **Coinmama** – It has 8 available cryptocurrencies in its selection, which include bitcoins. Coinmama requires a $60 minimum purchase. For each transaction, you will be charged a 5.9% transaction fee. If you're using a credit card for your purchase, you will be charged an additional 5% fee.

✓ **Gemini** – This crypto exchange offers bitcoin, bitcoin cash, and several altcoins. It requires users to purchase a minimum $60 purchase. The transaction fee for every transaction is 5.9% and an additional 5% fee if you purchase crypto using a credit card.

2. *Decentralized exchange* (DEXs)– These exchanges operate without any central authority and allow peer-to-peer trading. You can make transactions from your crypto wallet, directly sending or receiving crypto from another user. This eliminates the need to transfer assets to the platform, which lessens the risk of potential frauds and hacks. Technically, DEXs are pooled assets on the blockchain like Ethereum. One thing you need to know is you cannot trade Bitcoin on Ethereum-based assets. But you can select a pair of Bitcoin and Ethererum (or another altcoin).

This exchange type allows the smart contract to set the rules. A smart contract is technically a programming code that allows the system to execute transactions by itself.

For example, it automatically guarantees an Ethereum investor to obtain Bitcoin and vice-versa. Examples of decentralized exchange are *Ether Delta, PancakeSwap, Uniswap, and Bitshares* (BTS).

Table of comparison

	Crypto Exchange	Crypto Broker
Features	Best for average users	Best for experienced users
Use of fiat to buy crypto	Yes and No	Yes
Market depth	Limited market	Higher potential
Liquidity	Average level	Deeper level
Number of cryptos	High	Low
Safety	Funds are semi-protected	Protected
Regulations	Depending on your location	Regulated

Spread	Wide	Tight
Customer service	Limited only	Well-experienced

Other ways to get hold of Bitcoin

- ✓ **Peer-to-peer (P2P)** – It is the direct buying of bitcoins from owners who want to dispose of their holdings. You can check sellers from P2P exchange services such as LocalBitcoins.com, Bitquick, or Bisq. You need to create an account to post a request to obtain bitcoins. With the account, you can also sell your coins when you want to monetize them. Once your account is confirmed, you can start browsing the buy and sell listing offers and select a seller. However, you need to be extremely careful when opting for this option to avoid scammers. Only buy from legit sellers with positive reviews and high ratings.

- ✓ **Bitcoin ATMs** – Just like the conventional ATMs, they can be found in strategic places around the United States. They allow quick and hassle-free buying and selling bitcoins. It works by inserting cash into the machine to buy a certain amount of bitcoin. Once the transfer is confirmed, the coins will be transferred to the user's online wallet. However, using this option is more expensive since you will be charged with a purchase fee as well as a conversion fee (fiat to bitcoin). Typically, the average purchase fee is 8.4% of the amount you pay for bitcoins. While sales of bitcoins at ATMs are charged 5.4%.

✓ **Investment funds** – Digital currency asset manager Grayscale Investments offer Grayscale Bitcoin Trust (GBTC), letting you buy bitcoins from discount brokers.

✓ **Bitcoin futures** – It is for advanced investors who want to buy or sell bitcoins at a specific price on a future date.

✓ **Gift cards** – Gift cards can be traded for Bitcoin or used to purchase bitcoins. It works by buying a gift card from a retailer and logging in to any platform that accepts gift cards in exchange for bitcoins.

✓ **PayPal** – PayPal Holdings, Inc. (PYPL), a popular payment processor, is now offering Bitcoin. This option is safe and convenient because you can easily connect PayPal to your bank account or debit card or use the balance in your PayPal account to pay for your purchase from 3rd-party crypto providers. In addition, paying Bitcoin for the services or products you are purchasing is made possible via PayPal's "Checkout with Crypto" feature.

For a $100 to $200 crypto purchase, there is a $0.50 flat fee or a percentage of the total amount in dollars. The downside of buying Bitcoin or any crypto via PayPal is that it does not allow the transfer of bitcoins from its proprietary wallet to your personal wallet or an external wallet.

The transaction process: Deposits & Withdrawals

There are two ways to deposit and withdraw funds from the crypto exchange. One is using fiat currency and the second is cryptocurrency. But not all exchanges allow direct fiat deposit and only allow crypto deposits. Withdrawal and deposit fees are also higher when you use fiat. Crypto deposits have lower transaction fees.

Brokers usually offer a variety of deposit options such as cryptocurrencies, e-wallets, bank account, credit card, and debit card with no additional fees. For withdrawals, the fee is between 0% to 3% only.

The transaction fees

For every transaction, users need to pay fees which can be a percentage of the traded amount or a flat fee. Each crypto exchange or broker has its own transaction fees structure. Some of them charge higher withdrawal or trading fees or give discounts when you use their own token. Other exchanges based their fees on margin or a spread on top of the coin's market price.

Other factors that can influence the transaction fees are your payment method, location, security measures of the platform, and active trading features.

There are three fees to consider – deposit fees, trading fees, and withdrawal fees.

- **Deposit fees** depend on how you want to deposit your fund. Some exchanges do not charge bank transfers but charge a minimum of 3% of the amount to be traded when you use a debit or credit card for payment.

- **Withdrawal fees** typically depend on the percentage of the amount to be withdrawn or a flat fee.

- **Trading fees** are set by the exchange. There are also exchanges that publish their fees on their website while others would provide a quote during the trading.

Another factor to consider is the maker-taker fees of exchanges that offer active trading features. These fees are determined by price fluctuations in the crypto market.

If you set a certain price to buy a crypto and the market reaches that point, you will be charged with a "maker" fee. On the other hand, if you purchase coins at the prevailing market value, you will be charged with a "taker" fee which is higher than the other fee.

> ### PRO TIP
>
> *Check the type of fees that will be charged to you when you buy or sell your bitcoins before you sign up. It is also best to factor in the cost to prevent spending more than your budget.*

The sign-up process: Registration & Verification

Registering an account varies in *crypto exchanges*. There are platforms that only require a valid email address while others ask for additional verification proof like scanned ID, selfie while holding an ID, completing a KYC (know-your-client) process or even a video call.

It is the option by exchanges that accept fiat currency mode of payment and to confirm the request of clients who want a higher limit of withdrawal/deposit.

Verification of the account may take several hours after signing up or even a few days. Some exchanges have a longer verification period and others do not accept new accounts due to a long queue of requests.

The signup process with *brokers* is easy. However, they would require verification requirements since brokers' transactions are subject to regulations. For hassle-free validation, submit an ID and proof of current address like a utility bill. The verification process is quicker and once your account is verified, you can deposit funds and make some transactions.

The payment process: Connect your preferred payment option

Once the verification is complete, the exchange or broker system will ask you to connect a payment option (bank account, or debit/credit card).

You can also use your PayPal to buy bitcoins. There are two methods to get hold of Bitcoin through this payment processor. The first option is to use your PayPal account that is linked to your bank account or debit card. The second method is to buy Bitcoin from a 3rd-party provider and use the balance in your PayPal account to pay for it. However, only a few sites allow this option. Also, only 4 cryptocurrencies can be purchased through PayPal. They are Bitcoin, Litecoin, Bitcoin Cash, and Ethereum.

Is it safe to buy Bitcoin using credit cards?

There are two reasons why it is not advisable to use a credit card when purchasing bitcoins.

1. Not all crypto exchanges accept credit cards because of the risk of fraud and the higher processing fees. Transactions using credit cards necessitate paying additional charges, which the exchange will pass to users.

2. Purchases using credit cards are more expensive because the issuers consider the crypto purchase a cash advance transaction, hence charging higher interest rates and fees. In addition, there are credit card companies that limit bitcoin purchases to $1,000 per month.

Bitcoin investing 101: What do you need to start investing?

At this juncture, you have become more familiar with Bitcoin and crypto investing. Understanding how they work and paying extra consideration to risks and rewards are very vital to successful investing. Unlike the traditional financial instruments and equities, the value of Bitcoin is parallel to the people's interests. The higher the interest of investors, the bigger the demand that makes the price increase exponentially. Bitcoin has shown this phenomenon several times, creating new highs.

The basics are very simple. You just need the following to prepare:

- Secure internet connection
- Bank account information
- Personal identification documents
- Capital investment

Note: Personal and financial information is applicable when you are buying your coins from a crypto broker.

3 Popular strategies for investing in Bitcoin

Investing in Bitcoin is not very different from buying stocks and other financial assets. There are some similarities but also differences, in particular with the investment timeframes.

1. **Hold Bitcoin Long Term** – Some investors buy Bitcoin and want to hold them for a longer period because they believe that their value would appreciate in time or become a store of value like precious gold. However, these investors are inclined to sell their coins when they believe that the time is right and the returns satisfy their desire for profit.

2. **Buy and 'Hodl" Bitcoin** - The term 'hodl' is a misspelled hold, which originated from the bitcointalk forum in 2013 when one of the investors mistakenly typed in hodl rather than hold. He was saying implying to 'hold on for dear life.' It eventually became a popular investment philosophy and strategy that requires crypto investors not to sell their coins amidst price fluctuations.

   Hodlers are hard-core believers and maximalists. They believe that Bitcoin or other cryptocurrencies are here to replace fiat currencies in the long run. They do not do trading that is based on short-term swings of Bitcoin price. These investors simply hodl their bitcoins, avoiding the prognostication and volatility.

Moreover, they counteract the two destructive tendencies in investing – FOMO and FUD. Each represents a certain mental state and extreme emotions, causing a roller coaster of feelings that can help or hinder the success of traders/investors. Both have fear as the underlying emotion, which can be your best ally or worst enemy. FOMO is why prices go up and FUD is why the prices plunge.

- FOMO is the acronym for Fear of Missing Out. It leads investors to have a buying spree to avoid losing the golden opportunity. Somehow, the dominant emotions are making havoc over their prudence and logical reasoning. They disregard the possible dangers and are only focusing on the thought that they should buy right now!

- FUD is the acronym for Fear, Uncertainty, and Doubt. It leads to selling bitcoins at a low price. Sometimes it is called SODLing. The emotions typically come from negative or clickbait news and communication. A clickbait information is a calibrated message to generate traffic and also 'panic' among investors because of erroneous and shocking tactics. Most of the time, this misinformation comes from a bearish or confusing cryptocurrency market context.

3. **Trade Bitcoin based on their short-term volatility** – This strategy exposes the investors to greater risk but it offers faster compound profits. Bitcoin is volatile and is synonymous with unpredictable, violent valuation swings. Investors who enjoy short-term profits by buying coins on the dip and selling them at the peaks often go with this investing strategy.

In essence, it is a technique where investors hold on to their digital currency assets for less than one year and engage more often in buying and selling them. They are the 'active investors' who are targeting to earn huge profits in a short span of time. The downside of this strategy is the risk of losing a part of the investment if not careful.

This strategy requires knowledge, planning, and skills. You need to be aware of the fundamental principles, methods, and timing to make the trading experience rewarding in terms of financial and satisfaction aspects.

How long should you hold your Bitcoin?

The answer lies in your reasons and expectations. The primary goal of investment is to give you the opportunity to grow your finances by getting profits. Essentially, investing is a kind of business. You buy bitcoins during the bearish period and sell them when the market is bullish.

When you buy an asset, you typically choose a specific investment vehicle for one or more reasons. Perhaps you are investing because you are anticipating a big personal or family project 3 years from now. You want to have a consistent passive income or just to satisfy your speculation about this cryptocurrency.

People who invest in Bitcoin and other crypto enter the investing market with a vision to increase their net worth. Their goals keep them in the investment market even during bearish moments.

- Investors who invest in speculation do not observe a definite period to hold their investments. They can hold them for several hours, days, weeks, or even months before selling to the next investors who want to get hold of bitcoins and make future profits. These investors are always alert and would quickly sell the assets the moment they see that they would get a hefty ROI or buy more crypto.

- Investors who buy Bitcoin as a form of saving to finance a future project aim to sell the asset when it is time. The proceeds will be used solely for the special project. It doesn't matter so much if the amount of profit is not much as long as the intended amount for the project is covered.

- Investors buy Bitcoin as a source of consistent income. They hold their coins until the need comes and sell all or part of their crypto-asset to engage in another income-generating venture.

How long to hold your Bitcoin also depends on your perception of the crypto market. If there is continuing uncertainty and you are becoming anxious, you can decide to sell your investment and buy again in the future. There is no sense staying if you are emotionally down with the current downtrend scenarios. Besides, you can buy coins again during the bear period. In addition, if you already made a good profit and want to exit the market, then go for it. At the end of the day, always remember your investing goals and the reasons why you invest in Bitcoin.

When is the right time to buy Bitcoin?

Investor A purchased his Bitcoin a few days before the price in the market declined. Investor Z bought his Bitcoin when the price had gone to 50% of the original value and close to the period when the price became bullish.

The results?

- Investor Z made a 100% ROI of his investment because he bought the crypto asset at the right time.
- Investor A is still holding his Bitcoin and waiting for the price to go higher to earn a reasonable profit.

In retrospect:

The time you make an investment by buying your coin and how the crypto market behaves immediately after are other factors that will help you that influences the length of time you will hold your Bitcoin.

Therefore, your success is largely dependent on 'timing the market.' It means buying your coins when the price is low and selling them at the highest possible price when the market is strong. This is the simplest, yet most effective strategy. Never allow your emotions to overcome your logical reasoning.

Ways to Invest in Bitcoin

There are several direct and indirect methods to start investing in Bitcoin.

- **Buying and stockpiling Bitcoin**

    This is the simplest and fastest way to get hold of this crypto asset. Buying a standalone coin from a crypto exchange gives you ownership of Bitcoin. You can "physically" store your bitcoins in cold storage or use the encrypted wallet of the exchange platform.

- **Participating in mining Bitcoin**

    It means investing in companies that are involved in large-scale computing operations to mine Bitcoin. You earn profits and skip the complex part of the job.

    Another way is to let your computer be utilized as a public ledger node and receive Bitcoin for your participation.

- **Purchasing funds from Greyscale's Bitcoin Investment Trust (GBTC)**

    Greyscale offers investors to buy and hold Bitcoin in investor accounts, brokerage, Roth IRA, and certain IRA. This investment platform has made Bitcoin accessible to the masses, democratizing the notion that this popular crypto is for investors with huge capital. The funds offer diversification at relatively lower cost and allow investors to get exposure to the blockchain.

- **Buying shares in companies that use Bitcoin blockchain technology**

    In this method of Bitcoin investing, you are buying the corporate stocks of publicly traded companies that incorporate blockchain technology to complement their products or services or are focused on developing blockchain-based industrial infrastructures. It has been a hot option because of the crucial role of this innovative technology as the database for digital and crypto transactions.

Here are some companies offering stocks with underlying blockchain technology that you need to check out:

- ✓ **Amazon** – Aside from being the largest e-commerce platform in the world, it also operates the cloud infrastructure platform Amazon Web Services (AWS). This service allows clients to create their own blockchain network and manage them through Amazon Managed Blockchain.

- ✓ **CME Group** – Being the largest options exchange in the world that offers derivative securities for foreign exchange, indexes, and stocks, CME Group has also created an active Bitcoin futures contract market.

- ✓ **IBM** – IBM Blockchain has been providing transformative solutions to clients like True Tickets, Kroger, and a lot more. It helps customers establish dependable chains amidst the current pandemic and other challenging issues. Its AI and cloud initiatives also attract a considerable share of the information technology market.

✓ **Square** – The Cash App payment platform of this financial tech company offers peer-to-peer transactions that allow Bitcoin buying and selling much easier. During the 3rd quarter of 2020, about $1.6 billion worth of Bitcoin has been purchased through Cash App. Square also has established Square Crypto with a team of expert bitcoin developers with exciting projects under its sleeve like building open-source venture

✓ **Overstock.com Inc. (OSTK)** – This leading online retailer was among the first businesses that accepted Bitcoin payment. Its subsidiary Medici Ventures has been investing actively in projects that are blockchain-related for years. It also converted Medici as a fund that will be used to create blockchain startups. The fund has an 8-year timeframe and is managed by Pelion Venture Partners.

- ✓ **NVIDIA Corp (NVDA)** – This firm designs and creates high-end processing chips and graphic cards that are mostly used by supercomputers and servers of the crypto mining industry. It also produced exclusive chips for mining cryptocurrencies, offering more exposure to blockchain technology.

- ✓ **VMware Inc. (VMW)** – In 2020, the company successfully launched VMware Blockchain that helps clients manage extremely complicated workflows and multiparty applications.

- ✓ **Coinbase Global Inc. (COIN)** – COIN stocks have been on the high because of its great "cryptoeconomy" potential that is built on blockchain.

- **Investing in bitcoin futures ETFs**

Exchange-traded funds (ETFs) seem to be a safer option to invest your money. On October 19, 2021, the first SEC-approved bitcoin futures joined the ranks of other commodities or assets in the stock market. ProShares Bitcoin Strategy ETF BITO BITO tracks CME Bitcoin futures. During the futures contracts maturity, ProShares will collect a $95 (0.95%) fee for every $10,000 investment.

Key takeaways

- Several factors impact the value of Bitcoin- adoption as a payment system, store of value, finite supply, and reduced inflation.

- Getting started in Bitcoin investing is simple through crypto brokers or exchange platforms. The challenge is what kind of crypto to buy.

- Practicing safety measures, like getting cold storage (hardware wallets), is recommended to protect your Bitcoin.

- Investing in companies with Bitcoin in their hedge portfolio and using blockchain in their infrastructure or services is a viable option.

> **Point to Ponder**
>
> *One secret of successful investors is having a well-balanced crypto portfolio. Learn how to build one.*

Chapter 6

Personal Portfolio Management

"A good portfolio is more than a long list of stocks and bonds. It is a balanced whole with protections and opportunities with respect to a wide range of contingencies."
– Harry M. Markowitz
(Father of portfolio management and Nobel Prize-winning economist)-

A personal portfolio is a blueprint or a big-picture organized plan to manage the financial future. It is comprised of all the investments and a variety of asset classes you hold. A balanced, well-diversified personal portfolio is the key to financial freedom while your style of portfolio management will help you achieve it.

Portfolio management is about designing and managing the strategies to achieve the investment objectives. Essentially, the goals include getting a good deal of profits out of the acquired assets and asset allocation or choosing the type of investment vehicle that would give a short-term or long-term ROI.

Diversification is also a vital element to produce more income or hedge against inflation.

Investors who are fascinated with cryptocurrency added Bitcoin in their investment portfolio, whether through bitcoin futures ETF or blockchain-linked stocks.

Benefits of portfolio management

➤ It keeps the portfolio's performance in perspective.

➤ It helps you monitor the risk levels and rebalance your portfolio when necessary

➤ It guides you figure out your financial priorities.

➤ It helps you make regular investments to reach your investing goals faster.

What is portfolio management?

In a nutshell, portfolio management is the science and art of choosing investment assets and overseeing this group of investments to meet the financial goals and match the risk tolerance of the investor (individual, institution, or company).

It is about weighing the opportunities and threats or the strengths and weaknesses of different kinds of assets in the market to build a solid financial portfolio. Ultimately, the primary objective is to maximize the expected return of the investment within the set timeframe and risk exposure level. Investors can choose to manage their personal portfolios or hire a professional licensed portfolio manager.

Large investors usually have portfolio managers to take care of their portfolios. These managers use their market knowledge and professional skills to manage the portfolios with the help of software or apps that would simplify the process.

The crucial factors that they work on include:

- Average risk and reward by asset class
- Risks associated with the investments
- Risk measurement
- Understanding the investor's "risk tolerance"
- Relationship between risks and returns
- Returns correlations between assets
- Accounting for fees in planning the portfolio
- Options' valuation
- Diversification of portfolio

Different models of investment portfolios

Generally speaking, investors with bigger capital and want a long-time horizon would prefer to invest in high-return, high-risk options. Those with smaller investment funds and want a shorter time span would go for low-risk, low-return assets.

- ○ **Conservative portfolio** – This model allocates more funds to lower-risk assets (money market securities, fixed income securities). It aims to protect the portfolio's principal value hence being called sometimes a "capital preservation" portfolio.

  Opting for a conservative portfolio means that you are not totally avoiding the exposure to some growth stocks because they also help offset price inflation. You may choose to buy an index fund, equity from blockchain-linked companies, bitcoin futures contracts, and other alternative assets.

  Profile example:

  - ❖ 60% - 65% Equities
  - ❖ 25%-30% Fixed Income Securities
  - ❖ 5%-15% Cash and Equivalents

○ **Moderately conservative portfolio** – This kind of portfolio is ideal for investors who want to preserve the big part of the portfolio's total value but can take some level of risk. One strategy that works for this model is the current income where you invest in high-income securities such as coupon payments or dividends.
Profile example:

- ❖ 35% - 40% Equities
- ❖ 55%-60% Fixed Income Securities
- ❖ 5%-10% Cash and Equivalents

○ **Aggressive portfolio** – It has a higher volume of equities which means the portfolio value fluctuates day after day. The primary goal of an aggressive portfolio is to gain long-term capital growth. It uses a capital growth strategy to achieve the investor's goals. As for diversification, adding fixed-income securities is a good idea.

Profile example:

- ❖ 50% - 55% Equities
- ❖ 20%-25% Fixed Income Securities
- ❖ 5%-10% Cash and Equivalents

○ **Very aggressive portfolio** – This portfolio model is mainly composed of stocks. Investors who use a very aggressive portfolio aim for strong capital growth over a long-term period.

Profile example:

- ❖ 80% - 100% Equities
- ❖ 0%-10% Fixed Income Securities
- ❖ 0%-10% Cash and Equivalents

Remember that you can use them as a guide only and change the proportions of the assets to suit your preferences and investment needs.

Investment styles to consider for your portfolio

There are two primary types of portfolio management- active and passive. This is a fundamental decision to make as it will decide the direction of your investing success. If you choose this option, you believe that you can leverage the irregularities in market pricing and make excellent selections that are based not essential factors and not by chance.

1. Active portfolio management involves strategic planning when to buy or sell stocks and other forms of investment vehicles to beat the index performance.

- Investment funds that are actively managed typically have individual portfolio managers (team of managers or co-managers) who decide what to do with the assets. They use a combination of strategies, market forecasts, in-depth studies, and expertise to maximize the potential of the invested funds.

- Portfolio managers gather relevant data such as market trends, current news, political happenings that can affect the investment landscape, and economic situations. The irregularities can boost the potential ROI of the stocks and index funds.

- An active portfolio management approach uses brokers or fund managers to trade, buy, or sell stocks.

2. Passive portfolio management (also known as the set-it-and-forget-it strategy or an index fund management) duplicates the makeup of certain indexes to match their benchmark or market return. Investors who choose this option believe that investment markets are generally efficient and careful evaluation of available information about investment will lead to superior performance.

- It is ideal for people who prefer long-term investing in exchange-traded index funds.

- This strategy is structured like a mutual fund, a unit investment trust, or an exchange-traded fund (ETF).

- Passive portfolios have lower management fees compared to actively managed portfolios.

Factors to consider in portfolio management

1. Investment goals

The first order of business- you need to know your reasons why you invest your money. Investment goals generally center on the risk-return profile of the investors or how much risk and volatility they can withstand. Once the ideal level is reached, you can start formulating the winning strategies.

Here are some general questions to ask yourself when setting your objectives.

- What do you want to achieve within your timeframes?
- Are you hoping to preserve your wealth and make a legacy to guarantee a good future for your family?
- Do you want to build a solid portfolio that will replace your paycheck when you retire?

Setting your objectives is the fundamental starting point of investment. Goals are vital points when designing your initial personal portfolio. You can always modify them whenever necessary.

2. Asset allocation

Another crucial element in investing is selecting the asset classes that will make up the financial portfolio and how much is the budget allocation for individual vehicles.

Asset allocation is about having a good mix of bonds, stocks, "cash" (certificate of deposits), bitcoin futures ETFs, blockchain-linked stocks, and other alternative investments (derivatives, commodities, real estate) in your portfolio.

It provides balance and protection against the volatility of some assets. Generally, conservative investors would go for stable investments like stocks and bonds while the more aggressive ones are likely to combine growth stocks, crypto-based stocks, and other volatile investments.

- If your main goal is growth, you can invest in assets that are likely to appreciate and offer a hedge against inflation. Opting for a wider asset allocation lessens the risks while achieving your objectives.

- When your goal is enjoying short-term income from your investments, you may choose to select assets that yield fast ROI and profits. However, opting for all-- bonds or all-stocks portfolio may be a wise decision but over time, inflation can reduce your expected income. This can be resolved if you add other equities or assets that will protect your portfolio even if they do not directly generate income.

There are 6 common asset allocation strategies you can use to create a dynamic portfolio that brings beneficial overall returns:

a. *Strategic Asset Allocation* – It adheres to the principle of a proportional mixture of assets, taking into account the individual risk tolerance as well as time-frame. This method involves setting the targets and rebalancing the personal portfolio regularly to boost returns and cut back losses.

b. *Tactical Asset Allocation* – It is a tactical deviation within a short-term period that capitalizes or leverages the potential opportunities of exceptional investment. The flexibility would boost the market-timing aspect of the investment portfolio and rebalance the long-term positions of traditional assets.

c. *Insured Asset Allocation* – This method involves the creation of a base value that should be sustained. Investors or portfolio managers practice active portfolio management and rely on various resources (forecasts, analytical research, news, judgment, experiences) to make sound decisions when buying, selling, or holding assets. The insured asset allocation strategy is perfect for risk-averse people who want to secure their investments and achieve long-term goals.

d. *Constant-Weighting Asset Allocation* – This strategy adopts the approach of constant rebalancing of the portfolio. You purchase assets that have declined their value and sell them the value increases. The rule of thumb of this methodology is rebalancing when any of the asset classes show over a 5% deviation from the original value.

e. *Dynamic Asset Allocation* – It involves a constant adjustment of the mix of assets to adapt to the rise and fall of the markets. Technically, it is the opposite of the constant-weighting strategy because investors buy assets when their value increases and anticipate continued returns, and sell those with decreasing value in anticipation of possible further loss. Most of the time, the use of this strategy is influenced by the judgment of portfolio managers who speculate on the day-to-day performance of the assets.

f. *Integrated Asset Allocation* – It is a strategy that takes into consideration the risks of having a mix of assets and the expectations of market returns. In a sense, it encompasses all the key points of the other strategies.

3. Selection of uncorrelated assets

To reduce the risks in your personal portfolio, your best move is to diversify it by choosing uncorrelated assets. Overextended time, a lot of your accumulated assets may not be performing like before. By having a diversified portfolio of assets, you can attain your goals even if one of the asset classes did not perform well.

4. Tax implications

Investments are taxable so consider this when you are designing your personal portfolio. If you have diversified assets, they will be taxed accordingly depending on the classifications. This is where tax diversification comes in.

There are 3 "pools of money" in the United States – the taxable pool, the tax-deferred pool, and the tax-free pool. If your portfolio has a regular non-retirement account, traditional IRA, and Roth Ira, you have these three tax pools. A smart investor would always consider the tax implications to enjoy higher after-tax returns.

5. Diversification

The world of investing is uncertain. You may win or lose, which is why having a basket of investments that give you exposure to various asset classes would mitigate heavy loss. In essence, diversification spreads the risks and also the rewards within the asset classes. No one can accurately predict which assets would outperform the others, diversification will reduce volatility risk and cover the returns of all the subsets of assets or sectors over time.

5. Rebalancing

Rebalancing is simply the process of reverting the investment portfolio to the original asset allocation. It is typically conducted annually or at regular intervals. During the rebalancing, you can sell the high-priced assets and securities and buy lower-priced stocks or allocate the proceeds to bitcoin futures. Regular rebalancing will help you expand the growth opportunity and recapture the initial gains in potential sectors while keeping them aligned with your risk/return profile.

Phases of personal portfolio management

A. Planning

Like any kind of business, investing requires careful and smart planning. This initial stage of portfolio development requires making clear objectives, setting requirements, and selecting investment assets.

In determining the objectives, you should consider the returns after making investments, liquidity factors, time frame, and amount of risks. During this stage, scenarios like a market economy, inflation, changes in policies, regulations, and other vital factors should all be considered.

B. Implementing

When all the necessary requirements are set, the next step is implementing the chosen strategy. At this point, investors would be selecting the assets that would give them the rewards they want to achieve. Applying the diversification rule would help in minimizing the risks during financial crises and losses.

C. Controlling

Controlling means regular checking of the markets, doing analysis, and evaluating the portfolio's performance in the ever-changing investment climate. It also involves constant portfolio modification by selling overweight assets and buying underweight securities. While it can be challenging to make decisions due to the price fluctuations in the market, your experiences will help you master the strategies to effectively manage your personal portfolio.

Did you know that?

Genesis Mining company sent Bitcoin to a crypto wallet in the space via a P3P transaction.

When do you need a portfolio manager?

Outsourcing your portfolio management is an option if you are a busy person but want to gain exposure to stock markets and crypto markets. A financial professional who is adept and well-experienced in handling money-related matters helps you jumpstart your investing journey without hassle.

You may wonder about the difference between a portfolio manager and an investment manager, which is another common title of a professional handling financial matters for individuals or companies.

- Investment managers/advisors have broader roles which include investment management, estate management, debt management, tax management, budgeting, retirement planning, and more.

- Portfolio managers are mainly focused on providing sound recommendations, support, documentation, and portfolio management. They understand the financial needs of their clients and create investment solutions to maximize profits while minimizing the risks.

A portfolio manager will do the following for you:

✓ Helps you select the right assets to customize your portfolio and suggests where to invest or avoid

- ✓ Tailor-made the portfolio to match your age, risk tolerance, income, expectations, and investment horizon

- ✓ Designs customized investment solutions for you by analyzing your background, capacity to invest, and earnings

- ✓ Makes you aware of the available investment tools and the benefits of every investment plan

- ✓ Helps you realize the advantages of investing in particular asset classes and alternative assets

- ✓ Provides professional and unbiased advice on market trends and asset allocation to help you decide

- ✓ Maintains and monitors your portfolio

- ✓ Submits reports on individual investment assets

- ✓ Takes daily trading decisions to meet your financial goals

- ✓ Works to rebalance the account to ensure that it aligns with your risk appetite and preferences

Portfolio managers earn through commissions or fee-only cost, which is typically between 3 to 4%. They do not charge a per hour rate, retainer fee, asset-based fee, or fixed compensation.

How to find the right portfolio manager?

When choosing the right personal portfolio manager, you need to exercise maximum caution by doing the following:

- ➤ Choose someone with deep knowledge about the existing investment plans, financial markets, policies, and risks.
- ➤ Check the trustworthiness of the portfolio manager and with a good background. It is necessary to make a character check to find out his reputation in the industry. You do not want your hard-earned cash to be at the mercy of a dishonest, unprofessional, and shady person.

- ➤ Beware of a person who tries to impress you with professional jargon and complex terminologies about investing. A good portfolio manager should not confuse the clients, but help them become knowledgeable about the rewards and risks of investing.

Managing your personal portfolio

If you don't like someone to handle your personal investment portfolio, you can always choose to do it yourself. However, you need to brush up on your knowledge and skills to ensure that you are doing everything right.

Step 1

The first thing to do is learn how to **create your personal portfolio**. It should reflect your investment goals, investment strategies and approaches, risk tolerance, and capital requirements. Every investor has a unique personal portfolio to match his future income needs.

- Evaluate your financial situation, resources, age, and time you can spend growing your investments.
- Determine your future income needs and objectives.
- Consider the level of your risk tolerance and stress meter. Investing is highly speculative and if your tolerance bar is low, you might end up not sleeping over

losses when the worst scenario comes along.

- Pick asset classes that are not high-risk if you are a newbie and diversify your portfolio.
- Understand the risk/return tradeoff principle, which means the greater the risks of securities, the higher the returns. But never invest blindly or just because of the potential returns. You should weigh your options and start small if you decide to invest in volatile assets.

Step 2

Next to portfolio creation and asset allocation is to **determine the capital** you need for the asset classes you have picked up. This will fulfill the strategies you set for asset allocation. Make time to study the potential, risks, reward, and nature of every asset you want to invest in.

- **Stocks**

  When stock picking, consider the vital factors to satisfy your objectives and make you comfortable with your choice. They are the stock type, market capitalization, and sector. Make a shortlist of your preferred stocks and analyze each one before going forward. Stocks are high-risk investments and work-intensive, which means you need to be updated with the current market trends and regularly monitor the changes in the valuation/price of your holdings.

Subclasses:

- *Large-cap stocks* are shares offered by companies with more than $10 billion market capitalization.
- *Mid-cap stocks* are shares from companies with a market capitalization that range between $2 billion to $10 billion.
- *Small-cap stocks* are shares issued by companies that have less than $2 billion market capitalization.

- **Bonds**

When selecting bonds, consider the type of bond, the interest-rate environment, maturity, coupon, as well as credit rating.

- **Mutual funds**

  They are baskets of asset classes that are professionally picked and handled by fund managers.

- **ETFs (Exchange-traded funds)**

  In essence, ETFs are also mutual funds but they are traded like stocks. Both represent a group of stocks or index funds by market cap sector, location, and types. However, ETFs are not actively managed by fund managers, instead track a basket of stocks or a particular index.

- **Equities**

  Equities in investing are company stocks or shares. When you buy a share of stocks, you are technically getting a stake on the ownership interest or a fractional portion. You buy equities with the expectation that you will be earning capital gains when the value of the investment increase. Examples of equities are common stocks, preferred stocks, and treasury stocks.

- **Derivatives**

  The derivatives are complex securities whose value is determined or dependent on their underlying assets or benchmarks. They are actually a form of advanced investing with agreed-upon contracts between the provider and the investor. The common examples of derivatives in investing are futures contracts, options, forward contracts, warrants, and swaps.

- **Alternative investments**

  They are the asset classes that are not included in the traditional list of investment vehicles. They include cryptocurrency, real estate, precious stones, gold/silver, venture capital/private equity, oil, managed futures, hedge funds, antiques, commodities, wine, and artwork. Gold is the most preferred tangible inflation hedge because of its long-term store of value and liquidity.

  Alternative investments are usually favored by investors because they are excellent tools for personal or institutional portfolio diversification. Investing in hard assets (real estate property, gold, oil) is considered an effective hedge against inflation. They have a low correlation with bond and stock markets, typically moving on the opposite or counter position. This is many private endowments, pension funds, and other institutional funds allocate a portion of their portfolios to alternative investments. Currently, a lot of large investors are accumulating cryptocurrencies, in particular, Bitcoin to diversify their investment pool.

These types of investments are subject to the review and approval of the Securities and Exchange Commission (SEC). They also fall under the purview of the Consumer Protection Act and the Dodd-Frank Wall Street Reform. There are account providers that only offer this option to accredited investors. These investors have over $1 million net worth excluding their primary residential property or with at least $200,000 annual income.

Step 3

After establishing your personal portfolio, the next step is to periodically analyze, evaluate, and rebalance it. These tasks are crucial because the prices in the market are constantly moving, making a direct or indirect impact that changes your initial pool of assets.

Other elements that can alter the weightings of asset allocations over time are your risk tolerance, current financial situation, and future income needs.

- In terms of risk tolerance, perhaps you're more ready to invest in high-risk assets that offer greater rewards or your tolerance has dropped significantly and want to let go of some equities.

- Your financial situation also makes a difference. If you can afford to add more capital, start exploring other asset classes or alternative investments like Bitcoin. If you are still weighing the pros and cons of crypto investing, buying bitcoin futures ETFs is a good start.

Assessing the balance of your portfolio is important to know if the strategies are working favorably or you can still achieve your goals within the time frame you set. To determine the actual allocation of your investment vehicles, categorize them quantitatively and find out the value's proportion to the whole.

Step 4

The final task is rebalancing or adjusting the weightings of assets in your personal portfolio from time to time. It is done by selling and adding assets after evaluating which are in overweighted or underweighted positions.

- For instance, you have a 40% holding of small-cap equities but your asset allocation should only be 25%. You need to sell the exceeding volume and use the fund to buy other asset classes, probably a bitcoin futures contract or physical bitcoins and other alternative investments.

- Also, if you see that your growth stocks investment has appreciated over the past year beyond your expectations, you can stop adding a new asset class in this category. Selling your equity positions just to rebalance your financial portfolio would incur significant capital gain tax. The best decision is to balance it by adding other asset classes. However, if you think that your overweighted growth stocks would fall soon, selling them would mitigate a great loss.

How often do you need to rebalance your personal portfolio?

The frequency of rebalancing your investment portfolio will depend on the type of accounts you have, tax considerations, transaction costs, and personal preferences. An annual portfolio rebalancing is sufficient when there is no extraordinary growth appreciation anywhere in your portfolio assets.

The following general guidelines come in handy when you need to rebalance your portfolio:

> **Keep a record**.

Recording the cost of every security you bought and the total cost of your portfolio assets is important. The numbers will give you historical data that you can use to compare to future values of your portfolio, making it easy to see where to adjust.

➢ Compare the value

Anytime in the future, when you need to compare the values of the asset classes and the portfolio, you just need to review the record. To do the comparison, divide the current value of the individual asset class by the current total portfolio value. Find significant changes that may necessitate adjusting the assets allocation. But if you see that the figures are good and there is no urgent need for short-term liquidation of securities, then keep the original structure.

➢ Adjustment

If the weightings of some of your asset classes expose your personal portfolio to risk, make an adjustment. Simply get the current total value of the portfolio then multiply it individually on the original weightings assigned for each asset class. The results are the figures that you should invest in each class to revert back to the original allocation of assets.

How to measure your ROI?

The return of investment (ROI) measures the performance of any investment portfolio (personal, business, institutional).

The formula never changes: **ROI – (Gains-Cost)/Cost**

But ROI varies depending on the condition of the market and the type of securities/assets that investors hold.

When to sell or buy asset classes?

Timing is everything. Know when to sell your securities or buy new asset classes to balance your portfolio. Do not invest blindly, but always with a clear purpose. Never allow your emotions to influence your investing decisions. Reassess your purpose regularly to suit the market conditions and risks.

Key takeaways

- Building a profitable and winning portfolio requires learning the essential elements. Learn the art & science of investing.

- Be clear when establishing your investment goals.

- Diversification is not just owning different asset classes, but also spreading your securities holdings from each asset class to avoid exposure to great risks and volatility.

- Asset allocation is the basic investing principle in portfolio management because it helps investors to leverage the assets to gain maximum profits while minimizing various risks.

- Go for long-term investment if you want to earn compound interest, grow your investment, and avoid numerous transaction fees.

- Don't panic. Use the best strategy to mitigate losses. Remember that every asset has a good and bad time that may affect the weightings of your portfolio.

- Patience is a virtue when it comes to investing.

Point to Ponder

Never put all your investment eggs in one particular asset just because it is the current hottest investment vehicle and everyone is buying it.

Chapter 7

What Should Comprise Your Crypto Portfolio?

"With DeFi, we are building the finance system of tomorrow."
— Olawale Daniel-

Cryptocurrency is the new breed of asset class with a characteristic of higher risk and higher returns. The strong interest and global adoption of Bitcoin and other alternative coins make it possible for crypto to merit inclusion in the portfolio of investors and even in the traditional stock market.

While investing is subjective and the portfolio depends on the financial need as well as risk appetite, striking a balance is crucial to protect the assets. Whether your goal is to purely invest in Bitcoin and other cryptocurrencies or want to include bitcoin-linked exchange-traded funds, creating a well-diversified portfolio is crucial to successful investing.

What makes a good crypto portfolio?

> A 2% bitcoin allocation to the overall personal portfolio is a safe start for beginners. Advanced investors that are more risk-tolerant and daring can allocate more than this figure.

> Bitcoin remains the leading crypto with more than a 40% share of cryptocurrency market capitalization. It means, the price movement of Bitcoin influences the other cryptocurrencies.

> If you're into crypto investing, the best way to begin is having 60% of Bitcoin in your portfolio, then Ethereum. A portfolio of 75% Bitcoin and 25% Ethereum is an ideal composition for risk-adjusted returns.

Pro tip: *Most alternative coins (altcoins) do not survive the 4-year cycle or halving of Bitcoin. During this cycle is the bear-and-bull market periods, which are characterized by massive growth (bull) and accumulation (bear) of bitcoins. As Bitcoin keeps its ground during these cycles, other coins lose their market value and get busted in a flash.*

The evolution of crypto

Cryptocurrency evolves from Bitcoin (pure crypto) to Ethereum (decentralized platform with a proprietary currency), and DeFi (decentralized finance that uses smart contracts).

- **Bitcoin in your personal portfolio**

    Regarded as the 'king' of cryptocurrency, Bitcoin is the most popular and widely-used virtual currency. People want to own this coin because it has a solid user/holder base. No wonder, investors call it 'digital gold' because it can be used for many digital transactions anywhere in the world. Bitcoin investors believe in its enormous ability to continue growing value because of the fixed supply which is capped below 21 million coins. It makes Bitcoin a highly-prized asset and worthy to be part of the investment portfolio.

    If you have a diversified investment portfolio and allocated a portion of it in Bitcoin, you understand its high risk-reward characteristic. You may consider your crypto capital as a fund that you can afford to lose and the other asset classes are the ones to give you good ROIs. Counter-balancing is important in investing, hence the need for asset diversification. Keeping high-risk asset classes to a minimum and having fixed deposits and securities would protect your portfolio when volatility strikes.

- ## Ethereum in your portfolio

Ethereum's native token Ether has also proven its value for long-term investment. Like Bitcoin, it has gained popularity because of the network effect where new investors want what old investors have. Aside from this, Ethereum has successfully established itself as a global computing platform with an ecosystem of decentralized applications or "dapps". It has supported other cryptocurrencies, letting them grow in terms of users and value.

As a platform, it uses 'smart contracts' and collects Ether in exchange for contract execution. As Ethereum becomes increasingly popular across the globe, Ether also gains more value and utility, resulting in its long-term and sustainable value. Investors are now looking closely at the ability of Ether to provide direct profit.

- DeFi in your portfolio

  The term "DeFi" or decentralized finance is one of the frequently-mentioned words in the financial markets. Since Bitcoin and other cryptocurrencies operate on a peer-to-peer basis, it is not surprising that DeFi becomes the next big thing in the investment world because of this feature.

What exactly is DeFi?

In the digital world, DeFi offers the convenience of doing transactions without the intervention of a third party. It delivers quicker transactions, eliminates the high cost of fees to the intermediaries, and allows investors complete control over their assets.

In a way, DeFi is similar to Bitcoin and other cryptocurrencies because of its decentralized nature. It achieves distributed consensus with the help of smart contracts on the blockchain. These smart contracts perform certain actions when the required conditions are met.

What makes DeFi different from other cryptocurrencies?

DeFi represents the third wave of cryptocurrency. It pivoted the future of the financial and economic world, just like the explosion of stock companies during the 16th and 17th centuries.

In essence, decentralized finance (DeFi)) delivers efficiency. One of the cores of economics is the ability of a product to efficiently convert work into output or stuff. The blockchain's new structure of issued crypto with smart contracts spurs this efficiency.

In addition to the efficient way to do the established things, DeFi also offers exciting new ways to complete tasks. At present, the next generation of financial institutions is being invented to provide an infrastructure system that is free from the common issues that plague financial services such as layers of cost, waste, redundancy, and more. Expect that DeFi will spawn new strands of functionality to any kind of business.

Why should you use DeFi?

1. It is the future of finance.

In a nutshell, blockchain technology has disrupted the system of traditional finance and DeFi is now disrupting blockchain in a good way by harnessing the power and efficiency of digital contracts. DeFi platforms have become a place to trade, save, lend, borrow, and earn interest without the hassle of bureaucracy. The high level of accessibility via the DeFi platform gives equal opportunity for people who cannot open bank accounts or get loans from financial institutions.

2. It redefines cryptocurrency.

DeFi tokens are utilized as a medium of transactions at a lower cost. The automation process that it offers becomes the foundation to easy access to crypto worldwide as well as transparency. The decentralized nature eliminates the barrier of entry that most countries put up against cryptocurrency. DeFi removes the limiting country-specific requirements for investors.

3. It is diversified.

With DeFi, you go beyond the traditional method of exchanging and storing tokens. It gives essence to true decentralization, removing the need for any authority to accept, restrict, approve, and monitor financial transactions.

4. It ditches the paperwork.

Blockchain processed the transactions that use smart contracts, eliminating the hassle and trail of paperwork. There is also no waiting period, unlike the conventional process that involves bank clearing of financial transactions.

5. It quickens the pace of transactions.

Without the waiting time for clearing or approval of authorized people to complete the transactions, DeFi has the advantage of a providing quick and smooth experience for investors.

6. It gets rid of middlemen.

With automated smart contracts on the blockchain, there is no need for mediators like lawyers to make an agreement between the involved parties.

7. It equalizes financial opportunities.

The DeFi platforms offer financial opportunities that are normally offered by banks, hedge funds, and major financial institutions. With Defi, individual investors can access them without the usual strict requirements.

8. It is immutable.

The blockchain's records are tamper-proof, making them safe from unscrupulous people. Once the transactions are completed, there is no way to modify or delete them from the ledger system.

What are the downsides of DeFi?

1. Complexity

Compared to centralized finance where the institutions basically do everything, DeFi requires more engagement from the investors. This complexity makes the conservative and passive investors

2. Scalability and liquidity

While the locked-in liquidity value of DeFi as of October 2021 is around $12.5 billion, this value is relatively little compared to the traditional system. DeFi has the perfect structure for a small number of users. The problem of liquidity happens when huge withdrawals are made.

3. Insurance

Most of the DeFi projects are not covered by insurance, which can pose a great risk for investors who preferred security to safeguard their investment.

Quick Facts

DeFi is designed to eliminate two basic risks: operational mistakes and fraud.

Several ways to make money with DeFi

Decentralized finance helps investors maximize the potential of their assets and earn passive income. The growing ecosystem of DeFi makes it more attractive to investors and businesses who want to leverage its functionality.

Here are some straightforward approaches:

- **Lending**

    Most of the DeFi platforms specialize in lending. Holders of tokens can stake them for lending to earn APY (annual percentage yield). It works by lending your virtual assets and locking them into smart contracts. The interest accrued will be distributed to the lenders by the smart contracts in proportion to the locked-in asset value.

    The funds are accessed by borrowers in the form of loan that requires them to lock up collateral. When they fail to pay the interests on the set date, the smart contract will automatically enforce repayment from the collateral.

- **Staking**

  Staking refers to the process of utilizing smart contracts to lock in the digital assets for an extended period. The idea is similar to the regular savings bank account where the staker's balance accrues interest. Once you deposited your share in the smart contract, you can periodically claim your rewards.

  As an incentive, investors earn a proportionate share from the generated revenue of the DeFi platform. The incentives are in the form of tokens (similar to your token or another type of token in the blockchain). Some platforms require a minimum stake amount and an extended period of investment.

- **Becoming a liquidity provider**

  In this method, you can contribute liquidity to DeFi platforms' liquidity pools that offer token pairs. If your portfolio has multiple cryptocurrencies, you can invest a certain amount in the trading pairs.

For example -

You want to invest $2,000 worth of assets, so you contribute $1,000 worth of bitcoin and $1,000 worth of Ethereum. Once you lock them into the pool, you will earn LP (liquidity provider) tokens. They represent the shares you have in the total liquidity pool. When you redeem the LP tokens, you will receive your invested money plus the generated revenues that they earn from the crypto pair.

The more they are traded, the more tokens you will earn. But if the value of one of the tokens in the pool fluctuates significantly, you will lose money via IL or impermanent loss.

- **Yield Farming**

  Yield farming or liquidity mining involves locking your digital assets to LP (liquidity pool) in exchange for the native token rewards. Most often these tokens hold the right to vote (governance tokens) and participate in the reforms of the protocol or platform. In case you want to redeem your LP tokens, you will get back your stake plus the accrued share of income.

- **Borrowing and lending**

  In this approach, you are going to borrow a coin or token from the DeFi platform and use them to earn rewards by investing it back on the same platform or another platform.

  Example:

  - You swap $2,000 worth of BTC for wBTC.
  - Next, you deposit it to earn a 0.5% APY.
  - Since you have a Bitcoin deposit, you can apply for a collateralized loan (for another coin or token) for up to 75% of the total value which is $1,500.

  In this example, you unlocked the 75% value of your Bitcoin and earn passive income while benefitting from the original asset's capital growth.

- **Leveraging Non-fungible tokens (NFTs)**

Non-fungible token (NFT) is a new concept in decentralized finance that refers to the digital asset whose value is locked into a physical or digital asset like real estate property, works of arts, videos, or music.

NFTs in DeFi serve as proof of digital art ownership. They can be used as collateral for loans. NFTs also offer investors fractional ownership of the items sold by creators. In a way, NFTs represent the modern-day collectibles.

- ➤ NFTs went mainstream when a collage of images from Beeple fetched $69.3 million at Christie's auction house. The digital artist's collection was the first-ever traded NTF work of art.

- ➤ Other NTFs versions of collectible assets that went viral were LeBron James video clip of his slam dunk (more than $200,000), Nyan Cat GIF ($600,000), and the first tweet of Jack Dorsey ($2.9 million).

- **Participating in No-Loss Games & Lotteries**

  DeFi features a No-loss lottery where players use stablecoins to buy tickets. All the participating tickets are put in a pool where one winner is randomly selected. The winner gets all the accrued profits of the games. Those who lose can buy more tickets to have chances of winning or get back their capital back.

Top 10 DeFi altcoins that are revolutionizing the world

With the increased adoption of decentralized finance (DeFi) and the preference of users to use smart contracts in the blockchain, DeFi altcoins and tokens have become more popular. They do not only offer speculative value but they earn real revenues and offer great utility in the crypto industry.

AAVE

Date of Release: November 2017

Market Cap: $3.6 billion

Market Price: $266.76 *(COINBASE)*

subject to change

AAVE is the "governance token" that powers Aave, the decentralized money market protocol that allows investors to deposit or borrow cryptocurrency. It is the native utility token of the protocol that gives a right to the holders to participate in the future of protocol governance. AAVE is generally safe since it is created on the Ethereum blockchain. It has raised more than $16 billion in Initial Coin Offering (ICO) and was on the 2020 Top 100 cryptocurrencies.

What are the uses of AAVE tokens?

- ✓ It can be used to earn rewards through staking.

- ✓ It can be posted as loan collateral.

- ✓ It offers advantages to users like free use of certain Aave services or discounts on fees.

- ✓ It is given to lenders who deposited their crypto in the lending pool as compensation.

- ✓ It can be liquidated when the system needs more capital.

Project: Aave DeFi Network

Aave is a P2P lending system that is Ethereum-based and utilizes smart contracts that automate loan transactions. It is regarded as the first-ever DeFi application that is developed. It is existed and thrived before decentralized finance becomes a mainstream concept.

At present, Aave exists in the algorithmic money market. It enables users to profit from their crypto by lending and receiving loans through pools. To protect the assets of the investors, Aave requires over-collateralization or locking-in collateral that is worth more than the amount of loan.

Lenders are given aTokens or symbolic tokens to recognize their participation when they deposited their cryptocurrency in the lending pools. If you deposit an Ether (ETH) for instance, you will receive an aETH. Once you withdraw your ETH from the pool, the aETH will be converted to ETH.

The recent introduction of Aave's flash loan is a game-changer in the DeFi industry as it allows borrowers to secure quick loans without posting collateral and pay it before the mining of the next block of Ethereum. It also launched the Aave Pro for institutionalized or organized investors.

Where to buy AAVE?

AAVE tokens can be purchased and traded on Binance, Uphold, Huobi Global, and other cryptocurrency exchanges.

How to store your AAVE tokens?

Storing AAVE is relatively simple. You just need to secure an ERC-20 compatible wallet like MyCrypto or My EtherWallet (MEW). If you want more secured storage, hardware wallets like Ledger Nano X and Ledger Nano S support this token.

Is AAVE good crypto for long-term investment?

In the DeFi industry, AAVE is one of the most promising long-term investment assets because its market value is increasing by the day.

> It is the world's 45th largest digital asset.

- Since June 2021, AAVE recorded at least $150 million daily trading volume.

- According to the expert analysts of the Economy Forecast Agency, AAVE's market price will reach $528 by the end of 2022 and $1,254 by the end of 2023.

- There is a high expectation that if AAVE commands a $1,000 price, it would be in the list of large-cap assets in due time. Large-cap assets are worth over $10 billion.

At the moment, AAVE is growing as one of the largest altcoins in terms of market capitalization. AAVE offers lucrative benefits for individual and institutional investors along with attractive interest rates. It is one of the top 30 digital assets in the world as it benefits from the success of the project behind it. With innovative and unique features that offer great returns on investment, a safe network environment, and strong fundamental/technical aspects, investing in Aave is a great option. Its protocol Aave is considered by crypto enthusiasts and traders as the world's cryptocurrency bank.

How to start investing in AAVE?

Step 1: Register in an exchange platform where you can buy, trade, or invest in AAVE.

Step 2: Wait for the verification of your account. You may be required to upload a valid identification card as part of the Knowing Your Customer (KYC) process.

Step 3: Deposit your funds. AAVE can be purchased with fiat currency or cryptocurrency.

Step 4: Explore the AAVE page of the exchange and start buying AAVEs. Buying transaction is easy and fast. Within minutes, you can view your AAVE coins in your account.

Who should include AAVE in their investment portfolios?

- **Value investors** – While value investing is usually linked with stocks, the growing popularity and value of cryptocurrencies and tokens make them strong tradable assets. The high potential of AAVE to command its trading price and other functions make it a good addition to your personal portfolio.
- **Growth investors** – AAVE is a relatively new trading asset that can help growth investors on their goal to increase capital over time. With its increasing market price, AAVE is a dynamic asset for long-term investing and promises 5 to 10 times of trading price.
- **Crypto traders** – With high market potential and solid project backup, AAVE

is a strong DeFi coin that offers multiple percentage swings that bring significant ROIs for cryptocurrency traders in the long and short-term horizons.

- **Day traders** – AAVE's volatility benefits active traders who execute multiple intraday strategies to earn profits from the traded asset. It is ideal for various trading strategies like Range Trading, Scalping, High-frequency trading, and News-based trading.

- **DeFi/Blockchain enthusiasts** – These investors understand how Aave protocols work and the great potential of AAVE as crypto. They know that including AAVE in their personal portfolios would be profitable in a long-term timeframe.

ADA

Date of Release: September 2017

Market Cap: $52 billion

Market Price: $ 1.56 *(COINBASE)*

subject to change

ADA is Cardano's native cryptocurrency. This decentralized, open-source crypto began in 2015 but started trading in 2017.

Uses of ADA tokens:

- It is used by Cardano as a currency to run smart contracts.
- It is used to store value.
- It is used to send and receive.
- It can be used as payment for transaction fees on the network.
- It is used for staking or participating in the network's consensus process. It gives you passive income as you earn network fees for validating network transactions.

Project: Cardano

Cardano is both a smart contract and crypto platform that aims to be the next-generation evolution of Ethereum. It has enough flexibility, scalability, and sustainability to allow assets exchange as well as the creation of a wide range of DeFI apps, games, new tokens, and more. The first official usage of Cardano happened in December 2017 where Greek student diplomas were stored and verified on its blockchain.

Cardano's blockchain has two layers:

1. **Cardano Settlement Layer (CSL)** – It stores the accounts and balances ledgers. Transactions in the network are validated in this layer by the Ouroboros consensus mechanism.
2. **Cardano Computing Layer (CCL)** – It is where the apps' computations are executed through smart contracts.

Its primary objective is to become the crypto's most environmentally-friendly blockchain platform. It is often referred to as the "Green Blockchain." It uses Ouroboros, a unique POS (proof-of-stake) consensus mechanism instead of the energy-intensive POW (proof-of-work) that Bitcoin and Ethereum are utilizing.

How to buy ADA?

Step 1: Create an account on a cryptocurrency exchange that allows LINK trading with other virtual currencies like Bitcoin or fiat currencies like US dollars.

Step 2: Deposit funds in the account via bank transfer, cryptocurrency from a crypto wallet, or pay using a debit/credit card.

Step 3: Look for the "Buy Crypto" function to buy LINK tokens.

Step4: Complete your LINK purchase and connect your crypto wallet where you can transfer your tokens.

The official desktop wallet for Cardano is Daedalus, which is an open-source crypto wallet for ADA. It is compatible with Mac and Windows. Other great software options are Exodus and Atomic wallets.

The best hardware wallets in conjunction with Adalite (the open-source, client-side wallet) are Ledger Nano X, Ledger Nano S, and TREZOR Model T.

Is ADA a good long-term investment?

While Cardano crypto is still at its early stage of development, its growing popularity and widespread adoption of the crypto community make it a very good investment asset. Experts in the industry believe that ADA will remain on the top list of cryptocurrencies in the future, becoming a fierce rival of Ether, EOS, and more.

This digital asset offers plenty of long-term strategies and use-cases that suggest its longevity in the market. The platform is data-driven, peer-reviewed, and transparent. With a systematic approach, the volatility is minimized. The future projects of Cardano include a peer-to-peer crypto trading platform, a digital art marketplace, and a platform that trades real-world assets and stocks in its blockchain.

Cardano may appear as a high-risk investment now but its several innovative projects and strength despite being relatively new in the industry would pay big dividends in the future. The long-term growth plan of Cardano is an indication of its sustainable value that will benefit investors.

Long-term investors of ADA enjoyed huge profits during the first half of 2021 when its value increases to over 610%. It means that a $1,000 investment would be worth $7,100.

Forecasts

> ➢ Wallet Investor predicts that ADA's average price would climb to $4.44 by 2022 and up to $4.98 in 2025.
> ➢ PricePrediction's estimate for ADA would be $2.66 in 2022, $7.68 in 2025, and $54.29 by 2030.

COMP

Date of Release: September 2018

Market Cap: $1.7 billion

Market Price: $275.85 *(COINBASE)*

subject to change

COMP is the native token of the Compound DeFi protocol. Launched in June 2020, it serves as the network's primary governance token. Anyone who holds this investment instrument can vote on crucial decisions of the protocol such as borrowing power, introduction of new collateral types, or interest rate models.

Why invest in COMP?

- ✓ It represents the holder's right to vote on important issues that will impact the protocol's environment. One COMP means one vote. Users with 1% of the total supply of COMP can submit proposals about the protocol's plans and vote for the proposals of other investors.

- ✓ It allows COMP holders to earn passive income.

- ✓ It is perfect for HODLers and investors who prefer long-term investing.

- ✓ Its protocol allows smart contract audits by third parties like Open Zeppelin and Trail of Bits to ensure the highest level of integrity and security.

- ✓ It is backed up by strong and solid teams, all working to innovate and improve the protocol's ecosystem.

- ✓ It is easily accessible, leveraging its value growth and liquidity role in the network.

✓ It is a very solid and legitimate crypto coin that can be found in the list of major exchange platforms including Coinbase, Binance, BitPanda, Gate.io, Uphold, and Kraken.

✓ It can be stored in all major hardware wallets like Ledger Nano.

✓ Its supply is capped at 10 million, making it a much-sought altcoin with potential value appreciation. At present, COMP has more than 6 million circulating tokens in the market.

✓ Its price history since its launching in September 2020 has shown progressive growth with over 145% year-to-date returns.

Project: Compound

Compound is another DeFi lending protocol that offers APY rewards to depositors of cryptocurrency assets. Investors can use their deposits as collateral to borrow another kind of cryptocurrency. This flexibility makes Compound a much-sought DeFi project in the industry. Just like Aave, it runs on the blockchain system of Ethereum.

This network started the current craze of decentralized finance and was also the first one to launch a yield farming strategy to the crypto market in 2020. The farming pools locked the crypto of investors and provide corresponding rewards in a shorter period. Rewards come in the form of tokens that can be converted into supported crypto assets in the system. All investors who contributed funds receive cTokens that can be used for staking, trading, and transferring their crypto.

Compound has revolutionized the crypto market by offering an open lending environment to users who want to invest or get a short-term loan. The decentralized nature of the system eliminates credit checks and facilitates easy funding, provided there is collateral.

This protocol also utilizes Bitcoin in the DeFi markets through WBTC (Wrapped Bitcoin), which is the locked Bitcoin ERC-20 representation. WBTC allows HODLers of bitcoins easy access to the decentralized finance sector. Recently, this new token was voted to function as collateral in the protocol. Bitcoin holders are now given another way to unlock their coins' value.

How to buy COMP?

Step 1: Open your online account with an exchange or crypto broker.

Step 2: Purchase a crypto wallet where you can transfer or store your COMP coins.

Step 3: Place your order to buy COMP. Depending on the exchange or broker, you can pay through bank transfer, PayPal or other payment services, or credit card.

Step 4: Wait for your order's fulfillment.

If your goal is to hold them in the long-term period, transfer your COMP tokens immediately in cold storage or hardware wallet to ensure protection against cyber theft.

Why should you include COMP in your portfolio?

In a nutshell, allocating a 1% portion of your investment portfolio to COMP gives you the opportunity to enjoy the coin's speculative value growth and take part in its future direction in the crypto market.

Adding COMP to your personal portfolio of investment is a smart decision as it gives you voting rights to participate in its future as well as earn passive income as long as you keep it in the DeFI network. Currently, COMP is the world's 69th largest digital asset.

Another way to earn ROIs from your COMP investment is to leverage its high volatility level by capitalizing on the crypto market's short-term price movements. Buying and selling your assets would give you profits.

Crypto experts believe that COMP is a smart investing vehicle with room for growth. With the substantial increase of the Compound's Total Value Locked feature (or the number of assets being staked in the protocol) which is currently at $9.5 billion, there is a high expectation that its price would increase exponentially.

Forecasts

> ➢ Digital Coin Price predicts that by the end of 2021, the market price of COMP would reach $512 per token. By 2022, it would be $663 and in 2025, the price of COMP would be $982.

> ➢ CoinPedia has a fearless forecast of $1,800 to $2,200 by the end of 2022.

> ➢ Coin Price Forecast has a more conservative forecast of $412 (2022) and $814 (2025).

UNI

UNI is the native governance token of Uniswap. It was introduced to the market in September 2020 at $2.94 and has skyrocketed to $39.52 in April 2021 (a 703% surge within four months).

What are the functions of UNI?

- It gives holders the right to vote on major changes and new improvements in the platform like fee structure modification and distribution method of minted tokens.

- It is used to sustain the liquidity of the network.

- It is used as payment for fees in the platform.

Project: Uniswap

Uniswap is a prominent DeFi network that runs on the Ethereum blockchain. It is known for being AMM (automated market maker) which solves the usual liquidity issues that Decentralized exchanges (DEXs) typically experience. Uniswap can process more than $10 billion worth of transactions in a week, gaining 50% of the DeFi market as it functions as a market maker.

Its proprietary AMM system provides pooled liquidity through token swapping. It offers full control over private keys, low transaction fees, user-friendly operations, and integration of external wallets.

With unique and innovative features, Uniswap turned out to be one of the millionaire makers in the crypto industry.

Currently, UNI is the 12th most valuable cryptocurrency. Its DeFi ecosystem is growing steadily as well as the adoption of investors and traders.

In terms of past price performance, UNI has displayed an 8,200%+ROI which increased the investors' confidence and trust.

How to buy UNI?

Step 1: Sign up in your chosen Uniswap cryptocurrency exchange or broker. An exchange will enable you to swap UNI with Bitcoin, Ethereum, or any crypto of your choice.

Step 2: Deposit funds in your online account.

Step 3: Look for Uniswap from the available cryptocurrencies on the platform.

Step 4: Enter the amount of UNI you like to purchase and click Buy Order.

Step 5: Confirm your order and pay using the options in the exchange.

Is UNI ideal for long-term investment?

UNI is regarded as a future-focused altcoin. It has a clear roadmap and solid whitepaper that details where it hopes to be and achieve in the long run. The primary goals of this DeFi project are to empower the developers as well as the liquidity providers (or investors).

Proof that is a good long-term investment is the fact that the project is currently headed by an Ethereum developer and backed up by Vitalik Buterin.

The market price of UNI is driven not by celebrity endorsements or social media pronouncements, but by practical elements like its significance in the decentralized finance (DeFi) ecosystem, decentralized exchange, revolutionary upgrades, and increasing mass adoption for the governance token.

Forecasts

> ➢ According to Wallet Investor, UNI is a great choice for long-term investment and has predicted that its market price would hit $101.42 in the next 12 months and in 5 years, a piece of UNI would be worth $380.13.

> ➢ DigitalCoin's forecast for UNI would be $49.89 by the end of 2021 and up to $98.0 in 2025.

> ➢ Longforecast believes that UNI's price by the end of the year is $45.39 and $51.65 in 2023.

Maker (MKR)

Date of Release: December 2017

Market Cap: $3 billion

Market Price: $ 3,021.76 *(COINBASE)*

subject to change

Maker is the governance token of MakerDAO, the decentralized platform that is powered by the Ethereum blockchain. It has shown an impressive price jump from $597.37 in January 2021 to a high of $4,943.66 in April. One of the reasons that triggered the price increase was the news that MakerDAO has minted $38,000 DAI coins as funding for a mortgage loan. This means that it is bringing the real estate sector to the decentralized finance ecosystem.

What are the functions of Maker?

- It gives holders voting rights to the protocol's key reforms.

- It supports the creation of DAI stablecoin on the Ethereum blockchain.

- It is used by the Maker ecosystem to govern and manage the stablecoin DAI.

- It functions as support crypto to ensure that DAI is pegged to the price of the dollar.

- It unlocks the potential of DeFi for everyone in the global marketplace.

- It has a unique feature known as a deflationary protocol that helps in maintaining the value over time.

Project: MakerDAO

MakerDAO is governed by the autonomous organization or community, making it truly a decentralized network. This DeFi lending platform operates on "overcollaterization" to eliminate the concerns about the wild price fluctuations.

By locking in the collateral into smart contracts, users can get newly-minted DAI tokens or borrow cryptocurrencies. It uses advanced smart contracts called Collateralized Debt Position (CPD). This unique contract is initiated whenever the user sends tokens to the platform to get hold of DAI tokens.

Another proof that MakerDAO is secure and stable is the presence of Ether as an additional backup to withstand the crazy fluctuations. At present, about 2.52% of Ether is locked into the network.

MakerDAO also holds the record of being the first DeFI protocol that was able to achieve a TVL (total value locked) of $1 billion in 2020.

How to buy MKR?

Step 1: Open an online account in the exchange or broker with available MKRs.

Step 2: Purchase a crypto wallet. You can also store your MKR coins in a hardware wallet to protect them from possible hacking.

Step 3: Look for Uniswap from the available cryptocurrencies on the platform.

Step 4: Make your purchase order.

Step 5: Wait for your purchased MKR to appear in your account.

Is MKR a good long-term investment?

MKR is both good for short-term and long-term investments. If you decide to be an active trader, you need to capitalize on short-term movements of crypto prices throughout the day. For this, you need to convert them into stablecoin to start trading. Once you decide to stop day trading because the crypto prices are falling, sell your coins and keep your profit.

If you prefer long-term investing, make sure to store your MKRs in cold storage with a private set of keys.

Forecasts

The prospect that Maker token will explode in terms of market cap, mass adoption, and popularity is attributed to the platform's reinforcement of gaming networks and acting as a credit scoring and lending platform for merchants.

> Trading Beats forecast for Maker's price in 2022 is $3,459 and a maximum price of $3,635 by 2023.

> Waller Investor predicts that the long-term increase of MKR value in 2026 would be as high as $18,490.60. A 5-year investment would give back a return of approximately 473.89%.

Solana (SOL)

Date of Release: February 2018

Market Cap: $66 billion

Market Price: $ 218.41 *(COINBASE)*

subject to change

SOL is the native coin of Solana, a DeFi network that operates as a cryptocurrency and a platform exchange. This token has its own growth pattern that is not associated with Bitcoin's price movements. It is listed as one of the 2021 top ten largest cryptocurrencies, surprising the crypto industry when its price went up 13,300% from January to November 2021

Uses of SOL

- It functions as a payment for transaction fees.

- It is used for staking.

- It serves as the protocol's governance token.

Project: Solana

Solana is primarily designed to rival and outpace Ethereum in speed and efficiency. With a growing network, thriving DeFi and NFT platforms, as well as teams of more than 400 developers, Solana is indeed a powerful Ethereum killer.

Its ability to process 50,000 transactions every second has defeated Ethereum's 15 transactions per second.

> - Ethereum uses a Proof-of-Work mechanism to validate its transaction. POW operates by mining or staking.
> - Solana combines Proof-of-Stake and the revolutionary Proof-of-History consensus mechanism to unlock the high transaction speed. POH time-stamped the transactions on the blockchain or

decentralized network, eliminating the need for all computers to relay messages or agree to complete the transaction.

How to buy SOL?

Step 1: Open an account in the crypto exchange that supports Solana.

Step 2: Deposit money or cryptocurrency in your account.

Step 3: Look for the "Buy Crypto" function to purchase the number of SOL tokens you want.

Step 4: Pay using your preferred payment method.

Step 5: Wait for your SOL to appear in your account.

Is SOL a good long-term investment?

Crypto analysts are very confident that SOL will continue performing well in the market because of the popularity of its blockchain technology. Currently, there are more than 500 dApps (decentralized applications) built into the system by independent developers. It includes NTF trade, dating services, DeFi services, lending and borrowing services, lotteries, Play-to-earn (P2E) games, and more.

All the applications require SOL to complete the transactions, which is the reason why its value soared incredibly. For investors who want to add an exciting and promising altcoin to their personal portfolio, the Solana token is a wise choice.

Despite the high volatility of SOL which can be attributed to being relatively new and is still a work in progress, crypto experts believe that it is worth holding in a long-term period. Based on the technical and fundamental analysis of its price in the next few years, SOL would continue enjoying its uptrends. By holding your altcoins in a 5-year timeframe, your investment would multiply many times when the projected price of over $1,000 per token happened.

Forecasts

> ➤ Coin Price Forecast predicts that before the end of 2021, SOL's price would reach $774, more than $3,412 in 2023, and by December 2025, it would hit above $12,000.
> ➤ Digital Coin Price believes that Solana would reach a high of $376.22 in 2022, above $450 in 2023, and up to $658 by 2025.
> ➤ Coinpedia forecasts that SOL would be above $300 by the end of 2021, over $500 by December 2022, and up to $1,000 in 2025.

LINK

Date of Release: November 2017

Market Cap: $12 billion

Market Price: $ 26.16 *(COINBASE)*

subject to change

LINK is the native token and backbone of Chainlink, a decentralized oracle network running in the Ethereum blockchain. It started trading in September 2020 and was originally created to help finance the project's growth.

Uses of LINK tokens:

- It is used by users to pay for the network's services.
- It resolves liquidity issues of the decentralized exchange (DEX).
- It enables the trading of DeFi tokens.
- It is given as an incentive to the nodes (global computer network) that are verifying transactions and working to deliver accurate data. Those who want to be a node and offer data to Chainlink must first stake LINK into asmart

265

contract. This is to ensure that they will provide false data or misbehave.

Project: Chainlink

Chainlink's decentralized oracles connect different data sources and off-block feeds to the smart contracts. It has two components that interact with each other- blockchain and off-chain. The blockchain sets the oracle needed by the smart contracts based on the requested parameters while the off-chain is the oracle nodes in the Ethereum network that collect the information that users want. The pooled data is then processed by the Chainlink software.

Technically, Chainlink supplies value to other projects in the blockchain space by offering real-world data. It connects a smart contract to any of the following:

- Another smart contract
- Bank payment systems
- Various API's
- External sources

Oracle transmits and reviews real-time data to the network's ecosystem, verifying that the smart contracts' conditions are fulfilled correctly. It acts as the middleware between parties during the transfer of data and is particularly useful in DeFi because the network needs reliable and accurate data from several sources to eliminate errors.

How to buy LINK?

Step 1: Create an account on a cryptocurrency exchange that allows LINK trading with other virtual currencies like Bitcoin or fiat currencies like US dollars.

Step 2: Deposit funds in the account via bank transfer, cryptocurrency from a crypto wallet, or pay using a debit/credit card.

Step 3: Look for the "Buy Crypto" function to buy LINK tokens.

Step4: Complete your LINK purchase and connect your crypto wallet where you can transfer your tokens.

Is LINK a good long-term investment?

LINK ranked 16th by market capitalization in October 2021. When it was first traded, the price of LINK was $0.126297 and after a week became $0.50. It reached an all-time high of $52.20 in May and then fell down. Currently, its trading value is around$26.

Based on the popularity that this token and the success that Chainlink's team has gained, the prospects of exponential growth are tremendous.

- ➤ Linkchain's recent partnership with the biggest names in the decentralized finance sector and integration with IBM and Microsoft made LINK more valuable and attractive to investors.
- ➤ Linkchain has assisted Goggle, Binance, AAVE, Gartner, and other big names in the industry.

Forecasts

- Trading Beast predicts that the price of LINK will be stable until the end of the year and will trade between $21.52 and $29.35 in 2022.
- Wallet Investor believes that LINK is a great long-term investment and its price will reach $45 by 2022 and $100 by 2025.
- The fearless forecast comes for Coinlikers, saying that based on the continued growth of Chainlink, LINK's price will be at $210 in 5 years. This means a tenfold increase annually, making it one of the DeFi altcoins to invest in.

ATOM

> **Date of Release**: March 2019
>
> **Market Cap**: $6.2 billion
>
> **Market Price**: $ 27.85 *(COINBASE)*
>
> *subject to change*

ATOM is the native cryptocurrency of Cosmos.

Uses of ATOM:

- Users stake ATOM to earn rewards.
- It is used to make the "Global Hub" secure.

Project: Cosmos

Cosmos is designed to become the "internet of blockchains" or the "blockchain of all blockchains." It allows developers to create their dedicated blockchains (or zones) and provides them with prebuilt modules that are customizable to suit certain use cases.

Compared to other DeFi projects, it has wider use cases. It resolves three particular issues that typically limit the crypto institution.

- **Usability** – The easy modular framework of the Cosmos platform allows developers to implement the blockchain system on their specific projects.
- **Scalability** – Cosmos uses the native Tendermint BFT (byzantine fault-tolerant) consensus mechanism for this purpose.
- **Compatibility** – The Inter-Blockchain Communication (IBC) protocol allows all independent blockchains to connect.

How to buy ATOM?

Step 1: Open an account.

Step 2: Buy a hardware wallet to store your ATOM securely.

Step 3: Make your purchase through exchange platforms that support Cosmos ATOM.

Step 4: Transfer your Cosmos to your wallet.

Is ATOM a good long-term investment?

Investing in ATOM is a wise financial decision not only because of its relatively low market price but also the positive growth that it has shown. Experts in the industry are confident that it is the right asset for investors who are eyeing long-term gains. Also, right now is the perfect opportunity to invest in ATOM as it continues bringing high yields to the holders.

It has now over 256 services and applications existing on the platform which translates to about $131 billion in assets under management. This makes the Cosmos ecosystem healthy and more exciting.

Forecasts

- ➤ Coin Arbitrage Bot believes that Cosmos crypto would be trading at $25.70 by 2022, $41.58 by the end of 2023, and $67.28 by 2024.
- ➤ Wallet Investor fearlessly predicts that the ATOM's average trading price in 2026 would range between $111.86 and $172.17.
- ➤ Coin Price Forecast forecasts that ATOM's market price would soar to $1,387.19 by 2030.

DOT

DOT is the Polkadot network's native currency that was rolled during the phased process. About 58% of the original supply was given to the investors during the token sales, 30% was allocated for the Web 3 Foundation's development and development, and the remaining 12% are for the future fundraising activities of the network.

Uses of DOT:

- It allows holders to participate in the platform's governance by voting on key matters like network upgrades, network fees, and adding parachains or new chains.

- It is used for adding new chains (multiple, customized chains) to the network. The tokens are bonded or locked for a specified period.
- It is used by users for staking.

Project: Polkadot

Polkadot is the brainchild of Ethereum's co-founder Gavin Wood. This ambitious project aims to transform the structure of the blockchain network. It was launched in 2016 and developed by Web3 Foundation. Polkadot operates like Ethereum, with a blockchain platform that runs decentralized applications at very high speed. But rather than a single blockchain, its operating system accommodates a network of diverse blockchains to form a single ecosystem that interacts with each other. The more users who create parallel chains, the faster the Polkadot's network becomes. This DeFi project can process up to 1000 transactions per second and does not require forks to initiate updates and system improvement.

Its architecture has four elements:

1. **Relay chain or the main chain**- It is the heart of the system, providing interoperability and consensus to existing blockchains.

2. **Parachains or parallelizable chains** – These are blockchains that connect to the system and operate on their own. Each one has its own functionality and token.
3. **Parathreads** – They are blockchains that are like parachains but are more cost-efficient because of the pay-as-you-go payment scheme.
4. **Bridges** – They create connections, allowing the users to transfer data or tokens between blockchains.

How to buy DOT?

Step 1: Purchase a Polkadot-compatible wallet then locate your DOT address.

Step 2: Register to online crypto exchanges like Binance or CEX.io.

Step 3: Deposit funds in form of cryptocurrency, fiat, or bank card.

Step 4: Buy the amount of DOT you need.

Step 5: Wait for the tokens to reflect in your wallet.

Is DOT a good long-term investment?

Polkadot is one of the largest cryptocurrencies by market capitalization and has proven to be a worthy rival of the Ethereum network. The market cap influences the dominance and popularity of cryptocurrency. A high market cap (over $10 billion) is relative to "safe to invest in" and reduces its volatility.

In terms of returns on investment, this over a year-old token has given the early investors 1000% of their invested money. Crypto experts believe that DOT is a great option for long-term investment. It has already shown its ability to resolve the interoperability issue. It is also backed by the industry's most experienced people which include developers who come from Parity Technologies, researchers from ETH Zurich and Inria Paris, and capital partner Polychain Capital.

Price forecasts

- ➢ Wallet Investor forecasts that the price of DOT will increase to $74.0 by 2022 and $94.73 by the end of 2025.
- ➢ Long Forecast believes that this token will be $19.03 in 2022 and the longer-term forecast will be around $19.50.
- ➢ Digital Coin predicts that the average price of DOT in 2022 would be $93.93 and up to $159.59 in 2025.

YFI

Date of Release: July 2020

Market Cap: $ 1.1 billion

Market Price: $29,085.68

subject to change

YFI powers Yearn. finance. This governance, Ethereum-based token is distributed to the users of the network but can be sold or bought like other types of crypto. It is recognized as one of the precious crypto coins in the market that offer high annual percentage yield (APY) to users.

Uses of YFI:

- It gives holders the right to vote on the changes to the operational model or structure of the protocol.
- It is used by users as yDAI, yUSDT, and yUSDC to executive transactions.
- It also helps the users to earn trading fees and lending fees.

Project: Yearn

Yearn. finance or yEarn is a service aggregator that focuses on borrowing, lending, and yield farming. It simplifies the task of depositing funds to various decentralized finance (DeFi) projects by offering a streamlined portal. The interface uses an advanced "yield farming" tool that automatically moves liquidity to the DeFi projects through smart contracts. This process enables investors to achieve maximum returns. In addition, the unique automation toolset helps investors to make decisions about where to invest their money by using a streamlined DeFi approach.

How to buy YFI?

Step 1: Find an exchange that supports YFI.

Step 2: Once you decide which exchange you want, make an account and wait for its verification.

Step 3: Deposit funds that you will use to buy YFI.

Step 4: Make a purchase.

Is YFI a good long-term investment?

YFI is indeed a good investment asset considering that it operates on the Ethereum blockchain, allowing users to maximize passive income by holding crypto assets. Industry experts are calling it a DeFi giant because it has attracted developers and investors who want to take to leverage its usability and profitability.

Price forecasts

- ➢ Wallet Investor predicts a long-term increase of $225, 342 by the end of 2026. It means that a 5-year investment would bring a return of about +621.18%.
- ➢ Long Forecast believes that there will be a bull ride in 2024 and YFI may be trading between $47,959 and $55,179. It may climb as high as $315,257 in 2025 if the uptrends will continue.
- ➢ GOV Capital believes that the future price of YFI would climb to $90,379 by the end of 2022.

Key takeaways

- Ideally, a good crypto portfolio has Bitcoin and Ethereum on it.

- A diversified crypto portfolio with Bitcoin, altcoin (top crypto other than bitcoin), and DeFi tokens optimize your profits.

- Decentralized finance (DeFi) is revolutionizing the world with its infrastructure that can host individual investors and provide quick, automated services via smart contracts.

- DeFi altcoins are backed up with revolutionary projects that are pushing initiatives and advancing the way to deliver financial equality.

Point to Ponder

Successful investors do not rely on luck. They observe, speculate, and leverage the tipping point of market trends.

Chapter 8

Everything You Need to Ask About Bitcoin & Resources for Bitcoin Investors

"Bitcoin is absolutely the Wild West of finance...It is the frontier. Huge amounts of wealth will be created and destroyed as this new landscape is mapped out." – *Erik Voorhees*-

Frequently Asked Questions

Why so Bitcoin possess value?

Bitcoin's value comes from being a form of money that people trust and accept as payment, an investment asset, or trading vehicle. It possesses the characteristics of money like portability, durability, scarcity, fungibility, recognizability, and divisibility.

What can Bitcoin do?

Bitcoin has successfully altered the financial landscape.

- It is a digital currency.

- It is known as a global reputation and identification application.
- It initiates contracts, trusts, and wills.
- It offers decentralized domain names.
- It has a voting mechanism.
- It is used for crowdfunding.
- It attracts future markets.
- It is a micro-tipper.
- It has the ability to do what the basic financial system can do.

Why should you trust Bitcoin?

While trust in Bitcoin is subjective based on the human faith in numbers, algorithms, and encryption, this crypto offers 3 technological freedom principles that speak of integrity:

- Open source code
- Decentralization
- Peer-to-peer technology

Is it easy to buy Bitcoin?

Bitcoin is everywhere, meaning it can be purchased from various sources like exchanges or brokerage services. Check out the list of Bitcoin sellers and pay for it using fiat currency, PayPal, debit or credit card, or bank transfer.

How to sell Bitcoin?

Bitcoin can be sold using different methods- online, on exchange platforms, or through peer- to-peer transactions. The process is similar to the buying process, but this time you are setting the price for your bitcoins.

Is Bitcoin truly anonymous?

Transactions in Bitcoin use public addresses, a long string of about 30 characters that are usually difficult to remember. While this address is publicly-viewable, it does not have any identifying information or name of the user. This is why Bitcoin is called an "anonymous currency," but publishing this address and re- using it many times anywhere can be associated with your real identity because of the pattern. Hence, it is recommended to use a new address for every transaction you make. For this purpose, use a modern software wallet that is designed to let you generate a new address for every transaction you make.

For this reason, industry experts said that calling Bitcoin "pseudonymous" is more accurate rather than anonymous. This means that someone who is adept at uncovering real identities can potentially uncover the person behind the public address.

Who is in charge of Bitcoin?

None. Bitcoin is a software protocol just like the email's SMTP and the internet's HTTP. No person, group of people, or authorities can exert influence on how Bitcoin functions. In essence, the users are the ones in charge of their bitcoins.

Do I need to buy a Bitcoin wallet?

Think of your Bitcoin wallet as a physical wallet to keep your cash. It secures your money, giving you peace of mind because you have it in your possession. There are many choices in the market now, but the best option, if you want to prevent online hacking or theft, is to hold your coins in a specialized hardware wallet that lets you keep the keys offline.

What Bitcoin is good for?

As *payment or medium of excha*nge, Bitcoin is better than gold. This is because bitcoin is transportable, divisible, and a fixed unit of account. Its massive potential as a *store of value* makes institutional and individual investors convert portions of their portfolios to Bitcoins for diversification and hedge purposes. Bitcoin has already unlocked the *financial sovereignty* of investors by giving them the ability to make transactions without the need for permission from outside authorities.

What can you buy with Bitcoin?

Bitcoin can be used to buy about anything now from goods like foods, electronics, clothing to real estate, cars, and investment assets.

Why does Bitcoin price move a lot?

The price of Bitcoin is subject to the supply and demand of the market forces, which are in turn influenced by the trends/news in the financial world and whims of speculators. This is the rationale behind the sudden movements of its price, causing sharp upward or downward motion.

How to track the price of Bitcoin?

If you want real-time price movements of Bitcoin, track them in the data charts of Bitcoin.com. Use the Instant Price Converter to convert the price of Bitcoin to your local currency.

Is it profitable to mine Bitcoin?

The answer can be yes or no. Gone are those days that mining Bitcoin is possible using GPU cards or desktop computers. It now takes specially-designed computers or ASICs (application-specific integrated circuits) to unlock proof-of-work algorithm. Take note that this kind of equipment consumes a large amount of energy that can diminish your profits.

How do Bitcoin transactions work?

Bitcoin transactions involve an input (sending address), the amount, and the output (receiving address). Using the corresponding private keys, the transactions will be sent and verified by the miners within the blockchain.

How long does it take for Bitcoin transactions to be confirmed?

The typical time is roughly 10 minutes but because of popularity growth, the confirmation time can be one hour or more. When after 72 hours, the transaction fails to get confirmation, the fund is returned to the sender's wallet.

Is Bitcoin legal?

Regulations vary in different nations and some even banned its use. While it is not regulated, the use of Bitcoin is not illegal in some jurisdictions but users need to comply with certain conditions.

Is Bitcoin for criminals?

Bitcoin is money and like any representation of money (cash, checks, credit cards) can be used for legal or illegal purposes. The anonymity and decentralization features of Bitcoin (also of other cryptos) make it an attractive tool for criminal syndicates who are into peddling drugs and illegal goods, cyber theft, and kidnapping for ransom.

It is speculated that about 1% to 3% of transactions in the blockchain are used for illicit transactions. There are also reports that it is used for money laundering. But this narrative does not mean that it is for criminal activities. The majority of crypto-related crimes are scams. This means that crypto like Bitcoin is not a haven of illegal financial dealings of criminals, but a medium to enable trackable, secure transactions.

Will Bitcoin crash?

Bitcoin is notoriously volatile, which means its price collapse is always a possible scenario. Its history has large highs and falls, so prepared for the loss and enjoy the profits during a bull period. What's great about Bitcoin, it rises phenomenally and crashes down badly then recovers strong.

Is Bitcoin mining a waste of materials?

Bitcoin mining is essential to sustain the transaction ledger or blockchain. It requires a large amount of electricity and leaves e-waste. According to reports, the yearly carbon footprint of bitcoin mining is as big as the metro area of London or Romania. Its e-waste production accounts for more than 24 kilotons, the same amount of electronic waste in the Netherlands. Miners are using specific hardware that usually becomes unusable after 18 months are thrown away. If not properly disposed of, the heavy metals and toxic chemicals can leak into the water supply and soil.

Is Bitcoin taxable?

Since Bitcoin does not possess a legal tender status, its tax liability will depend on the jurisdiction. It can be in the form of sales tax, capital gain tax, income tax, and other tax liability.

Can Bitcoin become worthless?

It is possible that Bitcoin will lose its worth due to competing currencies, technical failures, political issues, and so on. All forms of currency are not immune to hard times that can make them worthless. But as of now, there is enough room for Bitcoin to grow and no one can predict its future.

Is Bitcoin a bubble?

A bubble is the artificial over-valuation leading to sudden downward correction. Bitcoin's quick rise is not considered a bubble. The reasons for Bitcoin price changes are mostly due to the users' sentiments that are influenced by the following:

- Loss of confidence in Bitcoin
- Increased press releases that stimulate speculative notions about the crypto coin
- Fear of uncertainty
- Irrational greed and exuberance
- Huge difference between price and value of the coin that is determined by Bitcoin's fundamentals

Is Bitcoin a Ponzi scheme?

No. A Ponzi scheme is an intentional fraudulent investment that is designed to get the invested fund of participants, affecting the last line of investors. Bitcoin is a software project where nobody can make fraudulent representations about its transactions and investment returns.

Will the finite amount of Bitcoin become a limitation?

While Bitcoin has a cap of 21 million only, there will be no limitations in the transactions because bitcoins can be denominated into sub-units. One bitcoin equates to 1,000,000 bits.

What will happen to Bitcoin if there is a better cryptocurrency?

To date, Bitcoin remains the leading cryptocurrency in the market. It continues to dominate the scene. When its price moves, the other cryptocurrencies usually follow. Also, it has inspired the creation of alternative crypto or altcoins.

Is Bitcoin secure?

The protocol and cryptography of Bitcoin have a solid record of security. The rules of its technology are still the same after more than a decade of operations. This is a clear indication that it is well-designed with strong security measures in the structure. The security issues in the software are promptly fixed and give Bitcoin more maturity. In addition, the common vulnerability and security problems lie in the errors of users like losing their wallet's private keys.

Resources for a smart Bitcoin investing

1. Bitcoin.com

https://www.bitcoin.com/get-started/

2. Investopedia.com

https://www.investopedia.com/bitcoin-4689766

https://www.investopedia.com/articles/forex/081815/benefits-risks-trading-forex-bitcoin.asp

https://www.investopedia.com/articles/investing/082914/basics-buying-and-investing-bitcoin.asp

https://www.investopedia.com/articles/investing/012215/how-invest-bitcoin-exchange-futures.asp

3. Robo-Advisor Pros

https://www.roboadvisorpros.com/best-portfolio-management-software-for-investors/

4. Bitcoin.org

https://bitcoin.org/en/

5. Trading Education.com

https://trading-education.com/

6. Management Study Guide.com

https://www.managementstudyguide.com/security-analysis-and-portfolio-management.htm

7. The Motley Fool

https://www.fool.com/quote/crypto/btc/

https://www.fool.com/investing/stock-market/market-sectors/financials/cryptocurrency-stocks/

https://www.fool.com/investing/how-to-invest/etfs/

Conclusion

"You can't stop things like Bitcoin. It will be everywhere and the world will have to readjust." – *John MCaffe*

Thank you for reading my book **Bitcoin & Cryptocurrency Investing: Top 10 DeFi Altcoins to Change the World and Your Finances, Blockchain, Cold Storage, NFT & Mining Explained, Smart Contracts & Decentralized Finance for Swing Trading.**

If you are here, then you have digested every single piece of information from the 8 chapters. If you find them useful, let them be your guiding wisdom in your exciting, exhilarating, and challenging journey in crypto investing.

Today, Bitcoin is the most powerful digital asset in terms of market capitalization, value, popularity, unit of account, and store of value. Perhaps, even its creator Satoshi Nakamoto is surprised by what Bitcoin has achieved so far. Or maybe, he knew this all along because just like his mysterious persona that many wants to uncover, unlocking Bitcoin's capabilities is like opening a Pandora box.

The technology behind Bitcoin has also opened a plethora of opportunities for the Fintech industry, sparking a revolution of digital projects that unite virtual technology with the traditional forms of investing. Major financial institutions including banks are considering Bitcoin, blockchain, and other forms of crypto to scale up their services as well as safeguard their hedge funds.

You and I have a lot to gain from what is happening in the cryptocurrency world. Bitcoin is truly an incredible trailblazer asset. It has made its mark in the economy and becomes an instrument to certain global issues. Bitcoin is an enabler of functions, an instrument for monetary transfer, and a powerful asset of investment.

Chapter 1 Hail to the King of Crypto: Bitcoin provided a lot of information and insights about this cryptocurrency. You've learned how blockchain works to empower Bitcoin and how it inspired other developers to create their own virtual currency. The world of crypto has become an exciting battle of crypto coins and tokens that now account for hundreds of varieties, all aiming to become the next Bitcoin.

You've met the world's Bitcoin millionaires and billionaires in *Chapter 2 The Digital Gold Rush*. These people believed and trusted the potentials of Bitcoin. They leveraged its volatility, braving the risks, and are now enjoying the fruits of their investment.

Bitcoin has transformed the investment sector's landscape as institutional investors joined the retail investors on the bandwagon of the virtual currency world. This solidified the position of

Bitcoin in the financial realm, increasing its speculative value.

Your answer to my question in *Chapter 3 Is Crypto Investing for You?* is obvious now that you are here on the final pages. You are becoming more curious about what more I can share. And I say that you are ready for Bitcoin investing. However, it is important to learn more, read more, delve more to become a credible and successful player in crypto investment. The more informed and skilled you become, the higher your chances of enjoying the rewards and eliminating the risks.

In *Chapter 4 Bitcoin and Stock Market*, you've learned that Bitcoin-linked futures have succeeded to join the stock markets. Moreover, the growing list of payment services and technology companies that are using blockchain and cryptocurrencies to maximize their profits is providing more opportunities for retail and traditionalist investors to invest in Bitcoin, albeit indirectly.

Use the information you gained from *Chapter 5 Guide to Bitcoin Investing: Let's Gear You Up* to help you avoid the traps and pitfalls in crypto investing. Like any kind of investing, there are risks and rewards to consider. By knowing how to reduce the risks like portfolio diversification, starting small at the beginning of your journey to the investment world, and matching your risk tolerance with the investment option, you are good to go.

A good personal portfolio is always a diversified one. It is unwise to put all your money in a single investment asset. In *Chapter 6 Personal Portfolio Management,* you've learned how to manage your own portfolio or hire a competent portfolio manager to do it for you.

In *Chapter 7 What Should Comprise Your Crypto Portfolio?* you've identified the best cryptocurrencies to include in your investment coffer. Now that DeFi is revolutionizing the financial world, picking up any of the popular DeFi cryptos in the list I've suggested is the key to optimizing its benefits.

Are there lots of questions in your mind? It's fine because *Chapter 8 Everything You Need to Ask About Bitcoin & Resources for Bitcoin Investors* answers your questions about Bitcoin. The list of resources would also lead you to more answers and strategies in investing.

At this point, you are equipped with the knowledge about investing in Bitcoin. This is the initial step that every investor should take and master. Preparation is the key to winning and eliminating the traps. When you are mentally prepared, you are more observant and vigilant. You know how to avoid or reduce the risks that can eat up your investments. You know what and when to buy or sell your holdings and anticipate the best returns.

Balancing your portfolio is a good way to start. Bitcoin is always the winning asset, so it should be your primary asset plus Ethereum, and the DeFi altcoins that are now showing growth potentials. They are the safest in terms of survival and liquidity.

A lot of altcoins didn't survive the Bitcoin halvings, so you have to be smart and trust only the cryptocurrencies that can hold their ground through these cycles. Never invest in random cryptocurrencies or participate in ICOs no matter how tempting the returns they offer without studying the risks and rewards, the people behind the projects, and other important factors. Remember that when your money is involved, you want returns of investment not saying goodbye to it. Choose your assets wisely and apply the learnings you get from this book.

The past and present performance of Bitcoin has shown us that it is a powerful force in the digital world, so everyone is expecting how it will transform the landscape of the economy in the future. Will it remain the best and major crypto player in the next decade or will be it ousted by Ethereum or other altcoins? That's for us to find out.

Finally, I wish you success in your journey to Bitcoin and crypto investing. Analysts and experts in the industry are predicting that in the next 5 years, the overall market of long-term investors would grow 10x, hence the best time to position yourself and begin investing is right NOW.

Thank You

Thank you so much for purchasing my book.

You could have picked from dozens of other books, but you took a chance and chose this one.

So, THANK YOU for getting this book and for making it all the way to the end.

Before you go, I wanted to ask you for one small favour.

Could you please consider posting a review on the Amazon?

Posting a review is the best and easiest way to support the work of independent authors like me.

Your feedback will help me to keep writing the kind of books that will help you get the results you want. It would mean a lot to me to hear from you

CPSIA information can be obtained
at www.ICGtesting.com
Printed in the USA
BVHW091714060522
636309BV00010B/1130

9 781914 271953